PARADOXES OF EVERYDAY LIFE

Paradoxes of Everyday Life

A Psychoanalyst's Interpretations

by Milton R. Sapirstein, M.D.

In collaboration with Alis De Sola

RANDOM HOUSE · NEW YORK

Dedicated with love to my sons,

FRED AND VICTOR

Paradox: "A statement or proposition seemingly self-contradictory or absurd, and yet explicable as expressing a truth."—*The American College Dictionary*

This is a book of paradoxes—especially those of ordinary daily experience—studied from a psychoanalytic viewpoint.

Analysis has always been concerned with paradoxes. What, in fact, was more paradoxical than neurosis until Freud discovered the power of man's unconscious? Much of Freud's original impact was based on his understanding of the psychopathology of everyday life. Perhaps, in our interest in the profoundly complex aspects of human behavior, we have missed the significance of familiar situations and actions so frequent that they escape observation; so seemingly trivial at times that they do not command thoughtful attention. Yet they too may lead us back to the primary sources of man's difficulties.

I make no great claims here for original contributions to theory. My hope is that this material, in an unaccustomed presentation, will prove stimulating and enlightening to the reader. Obviously a great mass of accumulated psychiatric data has been exploited in the preparation of this book, and it would be impossible to list here the many writers to whom I am indebted. I should like, however, to express my appreciation to three people specifically: to my assistant, Billi Boros, for her painstaking and perceptive efforts; to my collaborator, Alis De Sola, for her consummate writing skill and her innumerable suggestions; and to my wife, Lillian, for her surpassing patience and helpfulness in the face of many paradoxes.

New York, N. Y.   MILTON R. SAPIRSTEIN, M.D.

CONTENTS

PARADOXES OF EVERYDAY LIFE

CHAPTER 1

Outcasts from Eden:

The Paradox of the Marriage Manual

A good way of wrecking a new marriage is to present either or both of its partners with a marriage manual. . . . Paradoxical? Yes . . . Wildly exaggerated? Not really. The truth is that these solemn treatises, written though they are with all the good will in the world, make unreliable guides for the young people who consult them. Much of their advice is based on erroneous assumptions about men and women and the standards they set are rarely attainable. In doing so, they may create emotional strains which aggravate the very problems they are designed to solve.

Unless they are protected by a sense of humor, even quite settled couples may feel a sense of unease, of dissatisfaction with themselves and each other, when exposed to the counsels of perfection in the manuals. Measured against so glowing an ideal, the reasonable happiness they have achieved seems tame and flat, somehow unworthy. I can fancy them, those earnest couples, gazing at each other with a wild surmise. Would life have been richer, more meaningful, with somebody else? Or are they both lacking, dull clods forever condemned to mediocrity? A couple thus jolted out of its accustomed serenity might well agree with the poet who said:

"Never, being damned, see Paradise.
The heart will sweeten at its look;
Nor hell was known, till Paradise
Our senses shook." *

It is, indeed, a sense-shaking paradise to which the manuals beckon the true believer in their precepts. And, as I said before, unattainable, men and women being what they are. Perhaps I should make one point clear at the outset. When a couple, in spite of the most heroic efforts, fails to achieve the idyllic and continuous bliss described in the *vade mecum,* both husband and wife are apt to feel guilty and defrauded. But, in the majority of cases, it is the husband who feels most guilty, the wife

* Leonie Adams, *Those Not Elect.* New York, Robert M. McBride & Co., 1925.

most defrauded. To understand why, we must go back to the latter part of the nineteenth century and the pioneering studies in sexual psychology written by Havelock Ellis.

The reason we must do so is that contemporary marriage manuals, even the most recent, are all in greater or less degree variations on a theme first made explicit by Ellis. And that theme, in turn, was predicated on the kind of marriage and the kind of sexual relations within marriage which were the rule in Victorian England. Ellis, whose mind was both stimulating and generous, was an ardent feminist, as eager to wake women from the sexual torpor of centuries as others were to see her take a place in the world at large. It was the duty of men, he felt, to make that awakening glorious. As late as 1933, when a short version * of his massive "Studies" was published, he declared:

"The chief reason why women are considered 'frigid' lies less in themselves than in men. It is evident throughout that while in men the sexual impulse tends to develop spontaneously and actively, in women, however powerful it may be latently and more or less subconsciously, its active manifestations need in the first place to be called out. That, in our society, is normally the husband's function to effect. It is his part to educate his wife in the life of sex; it is he who will make sex demands a conscious desire to her. If he, by his ignorance, prejudice, impatience or lack of insight fails to

* *Psychology of Sex*. New York, Emerson Books, 1933.

play his natural part, his wife may, by no defect of her own, be counted as 'frigid.' "

While Ellis was probably the first Anglo-Saxon of note to place his *imprimatur* upon this theory, and while he was primarily responsible for its subsequent wide circulation, similar views had long been expressed by continental writers, notably Balzac and Stendhal. (The latter, incidentally, in his "De l'Amour," proved no mean feminist himself, a champion of women's rights at a time and in a country where women themselves displayed little interest in the subject. Among the reasons which motivated his attitude, not the least was his belief that genuine love is only possible between two free human beings, not between master and slave.)

Let me repeat: Ellis and the other writers who shared his views were arguing within the framework of a specific cultural setting—the patriarchal society which was still dominant in the Western civilization of their day and whose origins go back to the earliest period of the Judaeo-Christian era. In such a society, sexual desire and sexual pleasure were regarded as masculine prerogatives; the majority of women were anaesthetic and the majority of men content to have them so. Faced with this overwhelming fact, reformers like Ellis not unnaturally generalized on the basis of the existing situation. This led them to overlook certain fundamental realities about men and women which are determined, not culturally, but by biological and psychological laws. It will be the purpose of this chapter to explain those laws and to show why the marriage manuals, which also largely ignore them, may do more harm than good.

But first let us set our problem in context. What is the purpose of marriage, in particular of monogamous marriage? Why was the institution adopted at all? In terms of instinctual sexual gratification, it certainly serves no vital need; it is quite possible and sometimes more agreeable to find such gratification outside of marriage. Other animals do very well without it and there are primitive human societies where the kind of marriage we are speaking of is unknown.

A brief note on animals is in order, if only for the benefit of sentimentalists. Where they have a family organization at all, the unit consists only of mother and children. The male parent is either absent altogether or around on a strictly temporary basis. Each litter, except where human beings intervene, has a new father. As for insects, the attempt to find in their lives analogies to the family as we know it bogs down hopelessly, since what organization they have is confined to communal groups. We may add that there is little basis for the popular belief that true love exists among birds; the belief itself is merely a projection of our romantic ideals. In sub-human primates, on the other hand, we do often find the kind of close attachment between individuals which approximates our fond desires. Nothing in their relationships, however, approaches the stability of the monogamous family unit.

There must be some very basic reason why human

beings have formed this very special type of social organization. The reason, which also accounts for so many other complexities of human behavior, is to be found in the long period during which the human infant is helplessly dependent on others for its very survival.

There is in all nature, probably, no more profound relationship than that which exists between the human mother and her child. That it should be so is a vital necessity; without that extended and reciprocal attachment, the race would die. The child's need for the mother is obvious. Not so obvious, but equally important, is the mother's need for the child. Bearing a child, caring for it, supervising its growth, are deeply satisfying experiences for a woman. In a sense, she is dependent on her child's dependence for her own full development.

Occasionally one comes across human females—powerful, instinctually archaic creatures—for whom their mate's function is over when once he has succeeded in impregnating them. But they are the exceptions. Most women feel unable to cope single-handed with their reproductive task; they need in their environment a supporting male figure who will provide, not only shelter and food and care, but emotional sustenance as well.

Women's preference for such a stable association is thus not hard to explain. But what about men? By entering into a monogamous relationship they seem to hamper themselves unnecessarily, limiting their freedom to roam and make love where they please, shouldering economic burdens, even, in times of great stress, diminishing their capacity for individual survival. Why do they do it? What prompts them?

Well, men were babies themselves once. Human babies. The prolonged dependency of that period in their lives, the deeply-rooted attachment to one woman—the nourishing and reassuring mother image—are never entirely outgrown. However swaggering and confident they are, however male, they cannot be altogether free and self-sufficient. Infantile memories haunt the depths of their being, memories of helplessness, of fear and pain and warmth and love, of home.

As I said before, there are many primitive peoples who know nothing of our kind of marriage. Their family groupings, while often complex, lack the cohesion and stability found in more developed and successful societies. From the cultural standpoint, they are weeds, persistent but valueless. Every major culture, every branch of the human species which has left its mark on the face of the earth, has been characterized by strong fixed family units. The strongest of them all, monogamy, reached its high point in the Judaeo-Christian culture of the West which ultimately imposed itself on the greater part of the world. Its energy should not surprise us. The more secure children are, the more effective will be their achievement in maturity. And monogamy provides maximum security for both mother and child.

But such security depends on the loyalty of the father and for that loyalty he exacted a price. It was woman

who, in the interest of her maternal role, paid it. Not
too willingly, perhaps, but in the course of long centuries of educational and social pressure, without too
much protest. The price was, until very recently, the
surrender of herself as a person and, more particularly,
the renunciation of her capacity for sexual enjoyment.

Why was such a fantastic sacrifice demanded of her?
Submissiveness is all very well but why should any man
regard frigidity in his wife as a value rather than a liabil-
ity? Is it simply to keep her from temptation, to insure
that her children cannot possibly have any other father
than himself? Probably not. A woman can be chaste and
virtuous without being cold. Is he still hunting then,
perhaps, for the lost mother image, the woman who, in
his infancy, seemed to belong only to him, who gave
everything and asked nothing in return?

That hopeless unremitting search may be a factor in
the situation but it does not tell the whole story. Underlying the strange preference of the patriarchal male
is his awareness—rarely acknowledged, not conscious
even, but existing just the same—of a basic biological
fact, the fact that women have a far greater sexual potential than men. If he wakes the sleeping giantess, she
may prove too much for him. Asleep or somnolent, on
the other hand, she is no threat.

The average healthy female—even in our own culture, where she is still relatively repressed—is capable
of much more sexual activity than she can possibly experience with any one man. She can function repeat-

edly, having no need, as he does, to manufacture fresh seminal and testicular fluid. Moreover, whether she is interested or not, she is always anatomically ready for the act of intercourse; nature has thriftily arranged that the one egg she produces per month should have every chance of being fertilized.

Man's lot is much more difficult. Before he can get going at all, he must first have an erection, and that in itself is a very complex phenomenon, with nothing automatic about it. Recent animal experiments indicate that, in males, sex performance depends upon the integrity of the entire nervous system. A small cerebral lesion is enough to cause impotence. On the other hand, relatively massive lesions in the female will not prevent her from functioning.

The difference in sexual potential is less apparent among animals because, in them, desire is closely linked to the reproductive function and determined by hormonal action which reaches its peak at periodic intervals. During the breeding season, the sexual desire of animals is almost uncontrollable; in between, it is at a minimum. Among human beings, desire has been divorced from reproduction and is largely dependent on psychic rather than hormonal influences. Many women, indeed, experience heightened desire after their menopause when they are no longer capable of bearing children.

To refute my thesis that women have by far the greater sexual potential, objectors will point to an indubitable fact: the existence of male polygamy, more precisely polygyny, among a large number of cultures less sexually inhibited than our own.

Let's take a brief look at these cultures. What strikes us immediately is that, while the possession of multiple wives may be socially approved, few men actually have more than one. The custom is usually restricted to the ruling groups, among whom it is a sign of prestige, or determined, as in China, by the desire for additional male progeny where the first wife has failed to fulfill it. An authority on the subject, Lowie, has this to say: "The sexual factor pure and simple is of course not to be wholly ignored . . . but everything goes to show that its influence on the development of polygyny is slight." *

Another writer, Linton, remarks: "A man who can support a conjugal group without help must be richer and more able than the average. Conversely, in a polygynous society, monogamous unions may mean loss of prestige. If a man has only one wife, it will be tacitly assumed that he is too poor to buy or support a second." †

Another argument generally cited to bolster belief in the sexual superiority of the male grows out of women's ability to endure, without difficulty, long periods of complete sexual deprivation. It is true, also,

* R. H. Lowie, "Primitive Society." New York, Liveright, 1920.
† R. Linton, "The Study of Man: An Introduction." New York, Appleton-Century, 1936.

that orgasm, the summit of sexual pleasure, is more easily inhibited in women than in men.

True, at least, in our society which is still, in many ways, bemused by its past. The great weight of the patriarchal tradition has by no means been altogether lifted. It conditions the thinking and emotional attitudes of even the most enlightened among us and never does it lie more heavily than when we are engaged in making love. Women, of course, are particularly oppressed by it. Let us not forget that, for thousands of years, the dominant male tried to convince his mate that she wasn't really interested in sex. Home, school and church cooperated in making the lesson stick. So, as a matter of fact, did the medical profession.

Listen, for a sample of its views, to Acton, an English physician generally regarded in his day as an expert on the subject. In the year 1875, less than a century ago, he made this astonishing assertion: "The majority of women, happily for society, are not much troubled with sexual feelings." It was, in his opinion, a "vile aspersion" to suppose women capable of desire. Moreover, he declared sternly, only "lascivious women" took any pleasure in the sexual act. Acton, we must assume, was a conventional scientist. But he spoke for his kind and in line with commonly-accepted belief.

Women, generally, would have been the last to challenge his statements. With such pressures impinging upon her from every side, the lustiest wench could not help being intimidated. She would do everything in her power to still the excitement of her body, to deny its claims and conceal them from others. The penalty for failure, after all, was social ostracism, exclusion from the ranks of respectable womankind.

Most women, probably, never had to face this painful issue. Human beings, like plants, can be twisted into strange shapes if their training begins early enough and is vigilantly supervised. They will accept their deformation as the natural state of affairs and even take pride in it, as Chinese women once did in their crippled feet. The sexual impulse is so peculiarly plastic that it lends itself readily to the educational process. Especially when that process is universal, affording no grounds for comparison or envy. Unrecognized, deprivation loses much of its sting.

Moreover, patriarchal society offered its women some very genuine advantages in return for their docility. Since they were helpless creatures by definition, some man had to look out for them—father, husband, brother, brother-in-law or remote cousin, as the case might be. They did not have to spend agonized hours wondering, as so many women do today, about their place in the scheme of things. Their role was clearly marked out for them and it involved no abrupt changes in mid-stream, from a career to domesticity or vice versa. No choice, no doubts, no internal struggles. Marriage, a home and children were at once every woman's goal and the only excuse she needed for existence. To get a husband re-

quired little individual effort on her part and, once she
got him, she was pretty sure to keep him. He might
stray but only as a tethered goat strays; it was a rare man
who dared to break the chain of convention that bound
him to home and family. The same society which denied
women any joy in sex also set limits to the sexual activity of men. In doing so, it fulfilled its major purpose
—to provide a stable environment and the utmost protection for children.

Were men content in such a cultural setting? Could
they achieve sexual satisfaction with a partner so deeply
repressed? Apparently. We must remember that they
expected no response from the woman and would probably have been alarmed and disgusted if they got it. A
response would have seemed to them unwomanly, if
not indeed "unnatural." A man so conditioned does not
think of the sex act as a means of impressing the woman
or ingratiating himself in her eyes. The pleasure he
derives from it is a private pleasure, exclusively his
own, and he will seek it as often and in such manner as
his needs dictate.

Biologically, and to some extent psychologically as
well, this kind of sexual pattern is in many ways suited
to the male constitution. When the man's desire is alone
consulted, when he sets the sexual pace, undistracted by
the effect he may be making on the woman, he is able
to function to the best of his capacity. Under these
circumstances, psychic impotence is practically non-
existent and other defects in performance are of no

great consequence, either to the man himself or his mate. As far as she is concerned, sex is a burden anyway and whatever mitigates it so much gain. Thus the man's unconscious dependency on the woman is not threatened; he can proceed on his lordly way without the fear that she may become disgruntled with him and, perhaps, look elsewhere for satisfaction.

This, in broad outline, was the relationship between the sexes when Havelock Ellis began his work. Major changes were impending, caused by shifts in the general culture, but their manifestations were as yet sporadic, their implications hardly conceivable. Psychoanalysis was in its infancy; many of its most searching insights were still buried under assumptions hoary with age and never critically appraised because they were embedded in the mentality of the researchers themselves. Nobody, to return to our subject, questioned the superiority of the male sexual impulse. How, indeed, could there be any doubt of it when women were so very passive, so much its mere victims?

To Ellis, this female thralldom seemed both repugnant and unnecessary. Correctly assessing the importance of social factors in the situation, he associated himself with the feminist movement of his time. Women, he agreed, should be given the opportunity to play a more active and meaningful role in society. But it was with their sexual liberation that he was primarily concerned and here he drove home forcefully the individual man's responsibility to his mate. "It is his part to

educate his wife in the life of sex; it is he who will make
sex demands a conscious desire to her." Ellis, we may
concede, was right on this point which still retains considerable validity. But he also said: "As desire is usually
more irregular and more capricious in the woman than
in the man, it is the wife who may properly be regarded
as the law-giver in this matter and the husband may find
his advantage in according her this privilege." Will he?
There's the rub.

Women are no longer the beaten and submissive
creatures they once were. They are capable of earning
their own living, they vote, they think for themselves
and they expect to find pleasure in sexual experience.
For the great majority of them, marriage has not ceased
to be the supreme goal but it is a very different kind
of marriage from that of their grandmothers. It can
hardly be called a patriarchal institution any more; the
husband's absolute predominance is a thing of the past.
Nor is it, for the woman, an all-absorbing career. Modern contraceptive methods have made it possible to
limit the number of her children; in caring for them,
schools have taken over many of her previous responsibilities; a host of ingenious devices reduce the burden
of house-keeping. She has time and energy for outside
activities. And if marriage itself becomes a kind of
prison-house, the door of divorce is wide open.

All these changes are reflected in the sexual relations
between men and women. They are freer and warmer
than they were, more deeply significant for both part-

ners. But it would be foolish to claim that they are better in every respect. Certainly, marriage is not as solidly based as it was formerly and this instability alone creates many problems.

Some of the difficulties faced by married couples today are no doubt due to the fact that, sexually as in other respects, we live in an age of transition. Our values are confused and old outmoded habits of thought cling to them like burrs. In training our children, for instance, we tend to be uncertain; while boys and girls are not as restricted sexually as they were before, as oppressed by mysterious taboos, they are still somewhat alienated from the sensations of their developing bodies. In progressive homes, there may be a good deal of verbal freedom but behavior patterns have altered very slightly, if at all. Sexual functioning is discouraged by even the most enlightened parents for some years after it has become biologically possible. I am not saying these restrictions are unnecessary. They do, however, make it very hard for young people to adjust to the kind of adult sexual life which has now become the ideal.

Take the young girl. She is a little less ignorant of the facts of life than her grandmother was but, emotionally, she may be just as inhibited and her apprehensions are apt to be considerably keener. There is, after all, so much more expected of her in a world where the vital passionate female has become every man's dream, and where a transcendent image of her is celebrated by all the persuasive devices of mass communication. The inhibited girl must somehow resolve herself into a reasonably convincing facsimile of that image. Timidity is out of fashion; coolness and excessive reserve deplored. The emphasis is on the "warm" woman.

Nowadays the most inexperienced girl is aware that some sexual interest on her part is necessary if she wants boys to find her desirable. Unless she can manage, at the very least, to pretend eagerness, she is likely to be left out in the cold. Her first encounters may be rather frightening; she has to cope simultaneously with the adolescent male and her own childhood fears, a battle on two fronts for which she is not well equipped. If, after a number of experiences, she remains unresponsive, a new fear assails her: is something lacking, is she cold, as a woman a potential failure? Such a fear, in our times, induces much the same kind of shame which her grandmother would have felt had she been considered "fast." A girl who has never been sexually responsive enters marriage with a good deal of trepidation.

If, on the other hand, she is easily aroused, her disturbance may be even greater. Our morality is still heavily weighted against premature sexual adventures. The too responsive girl may fear, with some justice, that her emotions will get out of control and doom her to a life of promiscuity.

In any case, and whatever the nature of her premarital activity, the girl cannot in any genuine sense prepare herself for marriage. Her sexual role in that relationship will be entirely new and largely dependent on the character and reactions of her husband.

He, too, we must remember, was an inhibited child. Like his sisters, like the woman he will one day marry, he has forgotten the intense drama of those early days, with its overweening desires, its terrors and the inevitable defeat which was its climax. If it emerges into consciousness at all, it will be in the form of obscure guilts and anxieties, irrational compulsions, a pervasive feeling of insecurity. Only those whom we call neurotic are incapacitated by these ghostly visitations but all of us are troubled to a greater or less extent.

That is true especially during the critical periods of our development. One of those periods is adolescence. Primitive peoples, closer to the instinctual sources of behavior, take great pains to prepare their boys for manhood, for the duties, sexual and otherwise, of their adult lives. We leave sexual indoctrination to the whim of the individual parent. So it is not surprising that a boy's first contacts are usually fumbling and unsatisfactory, marked by such deficiencies in performance as loss of erection or premature ejaculation. There are men in whom these deficiencies persist, who, through fear or lack of opportunity, fail to achieve sexual confidence.

Most men, however, make a tolerable adjustment, gaining experience in one way or another, through a series of affairs, a relationship with an older woman or, *faute de mieux,* with prostitutes. Exposed as they are to our sex-glorifying civilization, they are under considerable pressure to become adequate lovers before venturing into marriage. They know that the girl of their dreams will expect it of them. They themselves expect to derive much of their sexual enjoyment from gratifying her and comparing their capacity to do so with that of other men. It is at this stage in a young man's life that, lacking the counsel of more experienced contemporaries, he may turn to the manuals for advice.

If he does, he will undoubtedly encounter a much-quoted dictum of Balzac's: "In love—quite apart from the psychic element—woman is a harp who only yields her secrets of melody to the master who knows how to handle her."

Incentive enough, one might think. But Van der Velde, the Dutch gynecologist who wrote the most successful of all manuals, "Ideal Marriage," adds his own gloss to the text: "Who can play this delicate human harp aright, unless he knows all her chords, and all the tones and semitones of feeling? Only the genius—after long practice and many discords and mistakes." Should the young man become discouraged and abandon all thought of marriage, he is hardly to be blamed.

One further note before we take up the case of Ted and Sally, two young people in love with each other, newly married and fairly conversant with the literature. The average young man we have been discussing is convinced that his sex drive is superior to that of most females. In this conviction he has the support of tradition and of his own premarital experiences. Almost always, the sexual initiative is his; he pursues while the girl of his choice retreats or, at least, pretends to. Her greater reserve is partly the result of more profound inhibitions, more stringent taboos, but it is reinforced by her unwillingness to take the social risks involved in sexual activity outside of marriage, as well as by her wish to offer the man an incentive for marriage. Virginity still carries a premium.

Let us turn now to our young couple. They are attractive, popular and reasonably sure of themselves; both have hurdled successfully the trials, disappointments and dangers which are the lot of youth. Ted has had, over a period of years, some gratifying adventures. Though they were casual, short-range relationships, he has no real reason to question his sexual capacity. However, a trace of insecurity remains, aggravated at the moment by the fact that he is very much in love. He cannot bear the thought that he might, just possibly, not come up to Sally's expectations.

Sally has doubts of her own. For one thing, she is a virgin and, while she is eager to put an end to that state, she now wonders whether it would not have been better to do so earlier. Were her motives for abstaining valid, is she really as passionate as she thinks she is? And what about Ted? During their courtship, he has stirred her intensely but will he be able to fulfill her long-deferred dreams? These mixed reactions, half fearful, half pleasurable, Sally keeps to herself. She loves Ted, and whatever happens, she has no intention of hurting him.

Both Sally and Ted, as I said before, had dipped into the manuals. Thus they did not expect too much of their wedding-night and, in any case, things went rather well. Ted was gentle and Sally grateful. They felt very close to each other. They were sure that, before the honeymoon was over, they would reach the peaks of mutual exaltation they both so ardently desired.

But they didn't. While Sally was as responsive as any man could desire, she failed to reach orgasm. And, since they had agreed to be honest with each other, she confided this fact to Ted. He, in turn, remembering his homework, gave more and more time to the preliminary sexual play which the manuals recommend for bringing the wife to the proper pitch of excitement.

It was no use. They returned from a fairly protracted honeymoon still very much in love but deeply disturbed by what they assumed was a failure in their relationship, an inadequacy on the part of one or the other. Ted developed a tendency to brood, as well he might. The manuals place most of the blame on him. As, for instance, to quote Ellis again: "One fears that there is still too much truth in Balzac's saying that, in this matter, the husband is sometimes like an orangutang playing a violin. The violin remains 'anaesthetic' but it is probably not the violin's fault." Nevertheless, Ted could not help feeling occasional flashes

of resentment. There were those other women he had
made love to in the past, after all. They had not been
so hard to satisfy.

Sally meanwhile, also found something to mull over,
a liberally quoted statement of Stendhal's which reads:
"A 'cold' passionless woman is a woman who has not
yet met the man she is bound to love." Sally was not
cold, of course, far from it. She was a warm sweet loving
woman and her greatest desire, at this potentially critical moment in her marriage, was to reassure her husband. So she devised a stratagem. By deliberately over-
acting, by pretending transports which she did not feel,
she succeeded in making Ted believe that she was now
reaching orgastic climax.

In Sally's case, the deception had unexpected results.
She did finally have an orgasm, as she would probably
have done earlier if she had not been so anxious. It was
not her pretense that turned the psychological trick but
the fact that, by concentrating upon her husband and
the pleasure she could give him, she forgot to worry
about herself. The reaction is both as simple and as
complicated as that.

We could leave our hypothetical young couple at this
point—united in their new happiness, slowly adjusting
to each other and their life together—were it not for
the marriage manuals. Ted and Sally took them seriously, very seriously indeed. They were determined to
achieve nothing less than the "ideal marriage" Van der
Velde writes about. It was not enough to enjoy making

love and for Sally to have occasional orgasms. She must have them every time, and moreover her climax had to coincide with Ted's. As Van der Velde puts it:

"In normal and perfect coitus, mutual orgasms must be almost simultaneous; the usual procedure is that the man's ejaculation begins and sets the woman's acme of sensation in train at once. The time it takes for the sensation received by the woman to reach her central nervous system and translate itself into supreme delight is less than a second. Such is the marvellous rate of nervous transmission."

Now this, I submit, is nonsense. A lotus dream, infinitely appealing, the goal of all desire—but nonsense just the same. It is a poet speaking, not a scientist, not anybody who deals soberly with the limits of what is possible. To the best of my knowledge, the standard of mutual simultaneous orgasm—described as "normal" by Van der Velde—is attained, if at all, only in the rarest, most fortuitous circumstances. There are a great many happily married couples, men and women whose sexual relations are completely satisfactory, who have never once experienced it. Nor, I may add, felt its lack. For one thing, as any honest woman will admit, the onset of the man's orgasm does not set her own "in train at once." It just doesn't work that way. She has to have her orgasm before he does or, at least, to begin having it. In the latter case, the peak of sensation for each *may* coincide. But one does not, if one is wise, stake one's happiness on such chances.

Let us return to Ted and Sally, who have set their
hearts on achieving this delirious consummation without knowing what pitfalls beset their path. Earnestly,
though with some embarrassment—they were rather shy
young people, temperamentally not inclined to excess—
they embarked on a career of erotic experimentation
which might have been suitable for the nymphs and
satyrs of mythology but which was rather too strenuous
for a rising young advertising executive and his mate.
They were encouraged in this course by the manuals
which uniformly urge the most complete freedom and
"abandon" on the young couple, backing up their argument that unlimited variation is normal and "good"
with all sorts of impressive data gleaned from biology,
anthropology, ancient history and literature.

During those early hectic months, Ted played to the
hilt the legendary role of the rampant male and Sally,
for her part, abetted him at every turn. Not only did she
respond eagerly to his slightest overture; she would
often initiate the love-making, having been told by the
manuals to forego modesty and do everything possible
to stimulate herself and her husband. No houri in the
Moslem paradise could have been more artful, more
enticing. There were times when Ted looked back, with
astonishment and wistfulness, to the days of their honeymoon. The new untrammeled Sally was marvellous but
he could hardly recognize in her the girl he had married. He couldn't always keep up with her either.

He tried hard, of course. Uppermost in his thoughts

was the desire to please her, to gain the approval of this lovely and astonishing creature. Not only affection but what Van der Velde calls a "husband's interest and honor" dictated that he should, on every occasion, give her as much gratification as she gave him. The mentor's words, in this connection, are very solemn: "I would impress on all married men that every erotic stimulation of their wives that does not terminate in orgasm represents an injury, and repeated injuries of this kind lead to permanent, or very obstinate, damage to soul and body."

As time went on, however, Ted was less and less able to carry out the implied injunction. Disturbing things began to happen to him; he had bad headaches and his nights were haunted by distressing dreams. Dreams in which he missed trains perpetually or failed in some vital examination. He was gallant with Sally, he showered her with compliments and extravagant presents, he took her out dancing as he had done in their courtship but he could not for long cover up the change in himself and he avoided intimacy as much as he could. Her attempts to stimulate him only made things worse; the harder she tried, the more reluctant was his response. Sally cried often these days and was glad they had put off having a baby. She was sure Ted didn't love her any more, at least not *that* way. One day, shortly after their first anniversary, she borrowed some money, packed her bags, and took a plane for Reno. Ted did not attempt to stop the divorce. Wretched as he was, he could see no alternative. Deep down, he was even relieved.

What happened to our young couple? Why did their marriage go on the rocks? They were healthy, in love, compatible in temperament and filled with the best intentions toward each other. All the ingredients of a successful marriage were present in their case. Yet they failed. It was an unnecessary failure, based on ignorance of natural laws and compounded by bad advice, like a ship sailing into uncharted seas with a defective compass.

There is room for democracy in marriage but, as nature has arranged matters, the husband's enjoyment of the act has to take precedence over his efforts to please his wife. Otherwise, sooner or later, neither of them will have any pleasure at all. (The problem is peculiar to a long-term relationship where the partners share the same home and have regular contact with each other. It may not arise in extramarital affairs, whose circumstances give the man much more leeway. If he is not in the mood for dalliance, he can always find a pretext to break the date. Moreover, such affairs usually involve a high degree of sexual tension on both sides, a tension maintained by infrequency of contact, need for concealment and a variety of other factors.)

Why should the husband's pleasure be so crucial? Because, unless he is assured of it, the mechanism of the sex act is impeded and may even break down altogether. The man cannot simply give in to desire as the woman can; he must feel it actively if he is to set in motion the chain of nerve impulses which lead to erection, and if he is to maintain the erection long enough to enter the woman. As I said earlier, it is a complex process, involving the entire nervous system. Once a man is sufficiently aroused, however, he will almost invariably complete the sexual experience which culminates for him in the orgastic release of ejaculation. At that point, his partner's interest, or lack of it, no longer concerns him. Getting started is the difficulty.

It is true that his desire can be stimulated. But not at all times nor in all circumstances. The assumption, implicit in the manuals, that the male sex drive is unlimited is—and I cannot repeat this too often—untenable, a hangover from the days when the majority of women were genuinely frigid. Actually, the drive has very definite limits. In a situation of physical danger to the organism, it becomes inoperative. Or it may wither away, as Ted's did, under the blight of anxiety.

Let us review Ted's case. The anxiety, residually present in him as it is in most men, first became activated during his honeymoon. Sally's failure to achieve orgasm, not uncommon in an inexperienced girl, was blown up out of all proportion in their minds, shadowing the delight they might have found in each other. To Ted, it was especially damaging since it led to doubts about his sexual prowess and thus lowered his self-esteem. But a quicker reaction on Sally's part would only have postponed his troubles; he was in any case, as subsequent events proved, a candidate for anxiety.

Let us be fair. The manuals were not wholly to blame
for Ted's plight though they certainly aggravated it.
Given the sexual mores of our time—between which and
the manuals there is a reciprocating relationship—any
well-disposed man is similarly a candidate for anxiety.
That is because, to win approval from his mate, to ingratiate himself with her, he has subordinated his pleasure in the sex act to hers. The test of success is then *her*
gratification, a hazardous undertaking at best since
it places the man on trial and induces the kind of defensive reaction which may end by paralyzing desire.
But the situation becomes much worse when the woman's enjoyment is, as it were, standardized, when an
almost impossible state of simultaneous ecstasy is made
the criterion of gratification. Inevitably, the ideal collapses against the stubborn realities imposed by nature.
Crushed under the ruins, not infrequently, is the man's
desire.

The woman's does not succumb so readily. Once
aroused, as it was in Sally, it can take on anything a man
has to offer and more. It is interesting that Van der
Velde, who places so great a burden on the man, nevertheless concedes the superior sexual potentiality of
women: ". . . the sexual vigor, efficiency (and technically *tolerance*) of the healthy, erotically awakened
woman is very great; decidedly greater, indeed, than the
potency of the average man."

There, in those few words, is the explanation of what

happened to Ted and Sally. She simply had more of what it takes than he had. Their mutual failure to achieve the ideal did not overwhelm her; she would have kept on trying indefinitely. As it was, she tried too hard. Following the advice of the manuals, she never denied herself to him, never begged off even when she was not in the mood. It would have been better for Ted if she had. He would have felt less guilty and incompetent, less like an honorable dwarf mated with a giantess.

Instead, ashamed to admit that his sexual interest didn't match hers, he allowed Sally to set the pace in their relations. Temporarily, that is, since in the final analysis the pace-maker has to be the man's sexual potential. When it gives out, to put it crudely, there ain't nothing. Ted drove himself to the point where he could hardly function at all. That precipitated the disaster. Had he been honest and confided in Sally, they might still have worked things out between them. In the circumstances, how could she guess that, when he avoided her embraces, he was motivated by fear of failure, rather than indifference? So, being young, ignorant and fairly insecure herself, Sally could only conclude that he no longer loved her. The feeling of being unloved saps a woman's confidence in the same way that a man's is sapped by the feeling of sexual inadequacy.

The saddest part of the story is that Sally would have been willing, at all times, to settle for less. She enjoyed the sex act, with or without orgasm; she had done so from the beginning. The sense of closeness, the deep satisfaction of being wanted, possessed, by the man she loved, were of extraordinary value to her. They induced contentment and that relaxation of nerves and muscles which, according to the manuals, is only possible with orgasm.

The manuals are mistaken. Most happily married women would admit that orgasm, while delightful, is not always essential to their enjoyment of intercourse. A few say it is and, moreover, insist that they invariably reach it. I am inclined to regard such claims with considerable skepticism. In my experience, they don't stand up under really close questioning. Among the women who make them are some, as a matter of fact, who don't even know what an orgasm is. Others, in their anxiety to be considered "normal," deliberately misstate the case.

Nevertheless, the whole issue does raise an interesting question. Why is orgasm, admittedly the high point in sexual experience, so very much less frequent in women than in men? In discussing the question, it will become clear why the goal of mutual simultaneous orgasm is, for all practical purposes, unattainable.

The first and most basic reason is that the mature woman is always *physiologically* prepared for intercourse. But she does not have to be psychically prepared since lack of desire imposes no veto on function. Thus, her participation in the act may be purely passive, without interest or expectancy. In this connection, the manuals stress the crucial importance of preliminary sexual play, variations in position and so forth. There are times when they do serve to arouse the woman but there does not seem to be any real correlation between such activities and orgasm. Experienced women often develop a "feel" about this culminating moment; they can almost predict in advance whether or not they will experience it on any particular occasion.

It is possible that hormonal as well as psychic factors determine the degree of response. Research in this field indicates that desire fluctuates during the menstrual cycle, that the woman's sexual receptivity is influenced by the hormonal changes which take place at different stages of the cycle. Some workers maintain that receptivity is greatest when fertilization is most probable—around the time of ovulation between the menstrual periods. While these findings seem plausible from a biological standpoint, many women contradict them. They claim their desire is most intense during or immediately before and after menstruation, the period of least fertility. Nor do the findings explain the heightened desire felt by so many women after they have passed the menopause. All we can say at this time is that the matter is not yet fully understood.

Another reason why women have fewer orgasms than men is the difference in orgastic pattern between the sexes. The male pattern is reflex; with very rare exceptions, orgasm accompanies ejaculation. Nor is sexual intercourse necessary for release. The same reflex pattern—ejaculation plus orgasm—obtains in involuntary nocturnal emissions, masturbation and a variety of perversions. Moreover, as Kinsey has reported, the pattern is established early in life, reaching a peak of frequency during adolescence and thereafter declining slowly.

For the woman, on the other hand, orgasm appears to be an induced reaction, a complicated matter involving a shift of psychic attention and what can only be described as a learning process. It may take years to achieve and some women never achieve it at all. That is not, in the circumstances, surprising. For one thing, and it is not unimportant, the woman has far less opportunity for sexual practice than the man. She is usually more strictly inhibited, both in childhood and adolescence. Her genitals are less available for inspection and manipulation. She possesses at least two, and possibly more, primary erogenous zones and the problem of transferring orgastic sensation from clitoris to vagina may bedevil her all her life. According to Kinsey, her frequency curve does not reach its peak until she is in her late twenties. At this age, his statistics indicate, the average man and woman are approximately equal in orgastic capacity.

At this age, however, most men and women have been married for some time. The man is also, as a rule, some years older than his wife. Suppose she is twenty-two when they marry and he twenty-seven. She has only begun the slow upward climb to her peak while he, though already on his way down, is far ahead of her in orgastic capacity. But, by the time she reaches the peak, he is thirty-four years old and no longer, in the majority of instances, a match for her. At almost no point is it possible for their frequency curves to coincide. Taking this and all the other factors into consideration, it is apparent that the goal of mutual simultaneous orgasm is unlikely of attainment this side of paradise.

Giving up a dream, particularly so radiant a dream, is never easy. We cling to it wistfully, hoping that somehow we can make it come true. The demand for perfection lurks in us all, a relic from those infantile days when our wishes were magically gratified, when desire and fulfillment were one. But it is better to be realistic. In the long run, we shall be happier.

I may have given the impression that, men and women being what they are, happiness in marriage is a very risky proposition. It need not be if both partners face the biological facts of life and are honest with each other. Let us return for the last time to Ted and Sally, those casualties of the quest for an ideal marriage. How should they have handled their sexual problem?

In the first place, by not making it such an all-absorbing problem. Self-consciousness is the death of spontaneity and, without spontaneity, there is no delight. When young people are in love, they can learn to adjust to each other without continually taking notes and measuring themselves against an abstract formula. Bed is not the place for intellectual exercises.

All they had to know really is that orgasm in women is not an imperative, and that its absence will not damage the woman in any way nor, indeed, prevent her from enjoying intercourse. If Ted and Sally had realized this, they would probably have stopped worrying. Sally could have "given" Ted his pleasure, even at times when she was not in the mood, and he could have accepted her compliance without guilt. His performance, incidentally, would have improved greatly, to Sally's benefit as well as his own. His confidence in himself might have been built up to the point where he could occasionally engage in the sex act because *she* wanted it. But he would never have felt ashamed to confess that he wasn't up to it and Sally would not have regarded such a confession as weakness or inadequacy on his part. It would be acknowledged between them that the pace of their relations must be set by him. But it would also be acknowledged that Sally did not always have to give in to his desires and that her refusal did not imply that she was either "cold" or unloving. With such an understanding between them, they could have found deep satisfaction in each other and placed their sexual relations securely within the context of their mutually dependent needs.

Ted and Sally were not predestined casualties. They might have had a good life together.

CHAPTER 2

Enigma Within a Paradox:
The Neurotic Child
from the "Happy" Home

There is nothing quite so sad as a disturbed child. To see a small creature overburdened at the very beginning of its journey through life invariably arouses pity. It also arouses, in the trained observer, what is nowadays an almost automatic judgment: something is wrong at home. The child may be withdrawn or fiercely destructive, uncontrollable or frightened into a state of morbid compliance, too excited or too apathetic. These are all neurotic symptoms and—so deeply have psychoanalytic insights penetrated our social fabric—they are recognized as such not only by the psychiatrist but by the teacher, the social worker, the judge.

Neurosis, we have learned, begins at home. So, in attempting to help the young victim, one of our first steps is to explore the family situation. We come prepared, as I said, to find something wrong. Nothing so gross, necessarily, as a drunken and abusive father or a mother who flagrantly neglects her duties. But something—bad blood between the parents, perhaps, a stony chill in the atmosphere, the suffocating fog of over-protectiveness. Maladjustments like these, and many others, are a commonplace. In investigating the background of the disturbed child, they would not surprise us.

What does surprise and puzzle us is to find instead an apparently happy home, one where the parents love and respect both each other and their children, where they take their responsibilities seriously and where there are no unusual strains, like extreme poverty or illness, to deflect the course of normal development. What on earth can be the matter with a child who fails to flourish in such a favorable environment? Here, indeed, is a paradox. In these days, when the parents themselves have become so much more knowledgeable psychologically, it confronts us increasingly. How can we explain it?

There was no problem, of course, before Freud appeared upon the scene, before the revolutionary insights of psychoanalysis began to dominate our thinking about human beings. In those innocent days, nobody placed undue emphasis on the family climate as determining the emotional development of children. Incipient neurotic traits were not even recognized nor were they taken into account if, at a later date, the child's personality became seriously disordered. It was tragic, no doubt, to have one's own child so afflicted but it was a tragedy for which the parents could disclaim responsibility. The blow came, as it were, from without—from an unkind fate, from God or, at most, from some constitutional anomaly over which they, as individuals, had no control. Ignorance thus alleviated the anxiety which springs from a sense of personal guilt.

Moreover, since large families were the rule in those days, the failure represented by a blighted child was not so overwhelming to the parents. They could derive a sort of statistical comfort from the fact that, in any numerous group, the chances are that one or more of its members will fall by the wayside.

All these easy assumptions were shattered by psychoanalysis. Cause was linked to effect in exhaustive and convincing detail; chance and doom, those outposts of superstitious thinking, began to crumble under the impact of accumulating research. As adult neuroses were traced back, step by step, to the earliest periods of childhood, the human mind was revealed as a jungle in which primitive impulses fought for survival and the strangling vines of early emotional disorders arrested or impeded healthy growth. To make of that jungle a cultivated landscape was the primary function of education. And education, like neurosis, begins at home. The child's first and most vital conditioning is derived from the parents.

The effects of such conditioning cannot be predicted with mathematical certainty. A multiplicity of factors, including a large number of variables, is involved. It is true that extraordinary exceptions to the laws of psychodynamics crop up from time to time. They have been explained on a constitutional or hereditary basis, with unusual sources of strength making adjustment possible even in the most unpromising kind of environment or, conversely, unusual weaknesses leading to collapse in spite of what seem ideal opportunities for growth.

Unless there is incontestable proof, and there rarely is, I have a personal aversion to this type of explanation. In accounting for such a paradox as the neurotic child from the happy home, I am much more inclined to believe that hidden psychodynamic factors are at work, factors far more subtle than those commonly analyzed. Among the gravest, in their effect on the child, are distortions in the authority to which he is subjected.

The traditional home in our civilization was authoritarian in structure, with the father as its undisputed head, the mother his deputy in the more intimate affairs of the family, and the children adjusting more or less obediently to their subordinate roles. This patriarchal pattern had both social and religious sanction; it was an integral element in the Judaeo-Christian culture of the West. Even when it did not actually conform to fact, where the mother, say, was the dominant figure, the illusion of paternal pre-eminence was maintained. Clarence Day's "Life With Father" gives us an amusing example of this family convention. There we see the seemingly docile and light-headed Vinnie serenely ruling the roost without ever issuing a direct challenge to the authority of her formidable but easily-flummoxed husband.

Nevertheless, and especally in democratic America, the whole idea of parental authority *was* challenged. Long before the time of Freud, European observers had noted and commented disapprovingly on the freedom and lack of respect for their elders which characterized American children. This trend toward the dissipation of family authority was given new impetus by the spread of psychoanalytic concepts. In a nation founded in rebellion and dedicated to the proposition that all men, including children, are created equal, they fell on fertile soil. Gradually, family life became revolutionized. The dominating father, the nagging mother were now regarded as psychic villains and strict discipline gave way to greater permissiveness. No longer were natural impulses equated with original sin, nor was their expression forbidden. The unhampered child, it was felt, would find his own way to maturity, nurtured in the sun of indulgent parental love.

He cannot, of course. And the intolerance once directed toward the earlier authoritarianism is now under suspicion. There is a temptation, in dealing with the difficulties of family life, to blame them on too much love, too great indulgence, and on the methods of progressive education in general, with its emphasis upon the free development of the child. It has become increasingly fashionable to blame excessive permissiveness for everything that goes wrong in the home. Because one over-simplified formula—the removal of arbitrary authority—failed to solve all the emotional problems of childhood, a reaction has set in which threatens to produce even more unrealistic solutions.

Have we really gone too far in abandoning authoritarianism in the home? Or not far enough? Have we perhaps, in our attempt to be enlightened and reasonable, imposed upon the child authoritarian techniques more baffling and painful than the harsh "dos and don'ts" we formerly employed? And have we, as a result, so confused the child that, while he is as bound as he ever was, he is even less capable of healthy rebellion?

It would be so temptingly easy to answer in the affirmative and join the bandwagon of an attack against progressivism. Let us resist the temptation and try to understand the paradox rather than dismiss it.

Making terms with reality, with things as they are, is a full-time business for the child. It is not easy, it is a sort of anguish, to leave behind the omnipotent phantasies of infancy and adjust to a world which, as every child discovers sooner or later, is distinctly not his oyster. Yet, to live successfully, to become a person, he has to explore and understand this world, moving outwards from the fixed base of home, finding his way more and more confidently as the unknown becomes the known.

The child's task is enormously complicated if his home is *not* a fixed base, if his parents—the guides upon whom he must rely—are not too certain about their position or disagree with each other about the paths he should follow. This is the case where traditional authority has been dissipated but where no specific policy determines the outer limits of permissiveness. One parent, for instance, may think the other is too strict, too demanding and compensate with unwarranted laxity. I am not now speaking of an open difference of opinion between them, which may be healthy, but of a subtle unconscious undermining influence.

We frequently observe this situation in the families of respected public figures, such as judges, educators and psychiatrists, who set up lofty standards for the conduct of the household but are too remote from its daily life to implement their decisions. The mother, on the other hand, may pity the children for being lashed to what seems an almost unapproachable ideal and forgive, sometimes even encourage, their transgressions. As far as possible, she will conceal these misdeeds from the father, of whom she may be somewhat in awe herself.

Unconsciously, she makes herself the ringleader of the children's rebellion.

Such a combination of permissiveness and discipline on the part of the parents is far more disturbing to the child than harsh but consistent authority. It creates both confusion and distrust and may lead, in later years, to impulsive, irresponsible and even destructive behavior. According to Phyllis Greenacre, a home situation of this kind is a breeding-ground for psychopathic personalities.

Another source of deep confusion results from what we might call a change in the ground rules of the home. The parents' attitude toward their child is, in the earlier stages of his development, completely loving and indulgent. All goes well at first; the child is bright, verbal and vivacious. Then, usually between the ages of four and eight, he becomes "difficult"—aggressive, demanding and unable to bear the slightest frustration. Other persons observe caustically that the child has been "spoiled." The parents are troubled. Is the accusation just? Have they, with all their good intentions, succeeded only in damaging this young life? Guilt turns to panic, panic to blind action. Like a driver who shifts abruptly into reverse when he sees a stone wall looming ahead, they want only to undo what has been done. So they bear down upon their unfortunate offspring, hemming him in with all sorts of rules and restrictions. The child, accustomed as he has been to the utmost freedom, naturally resists, becoming more unmanageable than ever. He learns the meaning of punishment, a shocking experience. The blithe spirit is no more. In its place there is either an angry rebel, eventually defiant of all authority or, if the discipline is brutal enough, a crushed being, emotionally paralyzed.

Too many parents nowadays tend to follow this pattern. Overindulgent in the early years, they are not prepared to follow through. Left to himself, the child might have learned that other people are not going to be as tolerant as his mother and father and adapted his behavior accordingly. At the very least, he would not feel that he had been betrayed. An eight or ten-year-old cannot be induced by force to accept the values of conformity nor can he, at that age, tolerate a discipline never previously imposed. Authority, if it is to be successful, must be consistently exercised from the earliest years and applied with a steady pressure, increasing or decreasing gradually as circumstances and the child's own development warrant.

If we compare the democratic home with its authoritarian predecessor, its most striking feature appears to be the decline in the father's prestige. He who was once the Jehovah of the family cosmos—remote, awe-inspiring, at once law-giver and judge—has dwindled into a minor deity. Mother and children no longer tremble before him; as a matter of fact, he would be embarrassed if they did. He is a familiar figure around the house now, a good guy who helps out with dishes and diapers, plays games with the children and rarely stands on his dignity. Moreover, he would be the first to admit that, if his stature has diminished, there are definite compensations in his new role. Certainly it is more agreeable to be loved than feared. And there is a satisfaction to be gained from participating intimately in family matters, from mothering as well as fathering, which is rooted in the profoundest depths of the personality.

And, no question about it, the family as a whole has benefited too. Home is a warmer place than it was formerly, there is in it more trust, more candor, more sheer animal vitality. Fear bottles up a lot of energies. So does the strain of living up to an artificial pattern of behavior. Everybody is happier. But, paradoxically, the situation involves loss as well as gain. The deflation of the father may lead to serious maladjustments in the development of his children.

His sons, particularly, may suffer. To become men in their turn, they must have an effective masculine figure with which to identify. Only so can they resolve successfully the crucial conflict of the oedipal period when they must break away finally from the infantile needs and desires which cluster around the mother. If the father's image is weak or blurred, if he lacks authority, it is much harder for them to make that great renunciation. Fear of his contempt or anger plays a vital part in establishing the necessary inner controls. Pride in his strength, and identification with it—"I, too, am a man"—compensate the boy for the sacrifice of his childish phantasies and encourage him to embark upon his masculine destiny. Unless the choice is decisive, a more or less severe neurosis may result and, in extreme cases, a homosexual orientation.

The girl's problem, during this period, is complicated by her relation to her mother who is, for her as for her brothers, the first love object. Though she has been grievously disappointed by that maternal figure, her affections still cling to it. Unless she can now transfer them to her father, with confidence in his ability to make up the phantasied loss, her femininity is endangered. Thus, for a different reason, she also needs a strong father.

There are other possible disturbances. Without a morally decisive father to worry about, both boys and girls may anticipate maturity and branch out toward an independence for which they are not yet ready. This may express itself sexually as well as in the personality as a whole. Such precocious independence, while it has its advantages, involves a distinct risk. Freedom is a heady draught, too heady perhaps for the immature, as the statistics on teen-age crime and immorality indicate. The father who kept strict tab on his children, who insisted at all times on knowing where they were and what they were doing, may have caused some unhealthy inhibitions. But he did protect them from disaster.

Uncertainty in the relations between parents and children may stem from an uncertainty in the parents' relations with each other. In a democratic home, much of the authority formerly exercized by the husband has passed to his wife. It was not wrested from him; he conceded it willingly, acknowledging her primary responsibility in such matters as family finances and bringing up children. And, since he has usually read the same books, or been influenced by them anyway, he may be quite honestly convinced that she is doing a good job. Convinced, that is, on an intellectual level. Underneath, he may be seething with rage over his children's willful behavior, their lack of discipline and respect. His exasperation may very well be justified. It may even be shared by his wife who is probably exhausted and would welcome his help in controlling the situation. She does not ask for it because they have agreed that the job is hers and he refrains from comment for fear of offending her. Instead, he abandons what should be a shared responsibility, depriving his wife of support and his children of the guidance they need.

The problem of authority is obviously not simple. It is impossible to deny that the tight family unit of the past had many genuine values, not the least of them being the clear definition of masculine and feminine functions. For the child, there was something very reassuring in the old system, which permitted no confusion in the parental images; the mother was the cherishing and protecting figure while authority and leadership resided in the father. So much we can admit. But, before we settle back comfortably into reaction, let us remember that clear definitions are not necessarily correct. Nor are easy solutions.

It is not hard to see why a child may become neurotic when there are inconsistencies and gaps in the pattern of authority to which he is exposed. But he may be just as bewildered and unhappy when sufficient authority of any kind is lacking—when nobody, in other words, tells him what to do. There are devoted and conscientious parents who lean over backwards in their attempts not to smother the child's developing self. They consult his preferences at every turn, let him smash things if he feels like it, be as impudent and overbearing and crotchety as his mood dictates. The wear and tear on the parents is considerable, of course, but they are sustained by their lofty purpose which is to give the child confidence in himself and in their unwavering love for him.

Well, it works sometimes. Not often. Most children react as though the rug had been pulled out from under their feet. (As it has, metaphorically.) They grow distrustful and whiny. They fret. Or go into tantrums without any provocation. And they will *not* make up their minds. Instead, they literally beg to be told what food to eat, what suit to wear, what game to play. Far from relishing their freedom, they try desperately to escape from it. They become unmitigated nuisances.

Are these children, then, just naturally perverse? Not at all. In reacting in this way to excessive permissiveness, they are merely claiming their rights—to be guided, admonished, punished if need be. Apart from the possibility that they may not be up to making all the decisions forced upon them, there is a deeper motive for their behavior. Confused by the many impulses that swarm into their consciousness, sensing how precarious is their own hold on reality, they want to be taken in hand. And so they misinterpret their parents' indulgence. To them it seems not love, not kindness, but a vast indifference to their needs. If mama and papa really "cared," the children feel, they would help us to choose, show us when we're wrong, walk with us as we stumble through this wonderful but frightening maze.

The children, while mistaken, have a valid point. Too much freedom is as bad as too little. And, for an undeveloped personality, even a quite reasonable degree of choice, by adult standards, may prove too much. He cannot assimilate it and, if his danger signals are not heeded, he will end up by feeling unloved and unwanted—rejected by the very people whose object it was to demonstrate their boundless acceptance.

It is amazing how often, in a loving home, such feelings of rejection arise. Baffled parents occasionally become aware of the symptoms but they cannot, for the life of them, understand the cause. Sometimes, if the child seems terribly insecure, they will consult a psychiatrist and ask how it is possible that Mary—or Peter or Bob or Sally—should behave so peculiarly. There's no *reason,* they complain. We're so happy together and we love the children. We've always wanted them, right from the beginning. They're *necessary* to us. How can they not know it?

One simple but easily overlooked fact which is seen more frequently in the happy home may account for the child's apparently unmotivated fears. If the love between the parents is deep and passionate, their absorption in each other may convey itself to the child with such force that he feels like an interloper, an unwanted third party at the feast of love. Such scraps—to his mind—as they offer him are not enough. What he wants is a chance to break into the combine, to edge out his rival in the family romance; and this, their attitude makes clear, is impossible.

Normally, children enter the ocdipal situation with some hope, however vague, that they will succeed in displacing their father or mother, as the case may be, and win exclusive affection from the parent of the opposite sex. While these phantasies are doomed to frustration, they should be permitted their brief period of bloom; a child who cannot dream loses the capacity for healthy expectation. Moreover, by being disbarred in advance from the oedipal struggle, the child misses the opportunity—so vital for his character development—of voluntarily relinquishing dream for reality. Obviously, there is no virtue in renouncing what one has never even hoped to possess.

The inability to phantasy success in the oedipal situation may have serious consequences for the individual in later years. A sense of his own worth and desirability may be totally lacking. He avoids sexual competition, anticipating defeat at the first sign of a rival or—what is perhaps even worse—seeks out partners who reject and humiliate him. Both men and women suffer from this unconscious handicap but I have seen it most often in young girls with beautiful mothers. They take it for granted that their boy friends, like their fathers, will automatically prefer the mother to them. If they marry, they expect to lose their husbands to other more glamorous women. Very frequently they do, having in a sense predetermined the outcome. As George Sand observed in her autobiography, "It always happens that one gives form and substance to the dangers upon which one broods to excess."

Let me emphasize that these children are not really rejected by their parents. They may, indeed, receive more than the usual amount of love and attention. What scars them and sets the pattern for their future relationships is their feeling of exclusion from the family romance.

There is another home situation—analagous to the one I have just described, but having special features of its own—which may also result in unwarranted feelings of rejection. That is where the mother and father maintain an unshakeable "united front." They never quarrel in front of the children, never disagree, and support each other staunchly in every decision affecting their offspring. Parents of this type have usually been disturbed in childhood by conflicts between *their* parents and they are determined to protect their own children from such a potentially shattering experience.

So they do, but at a price. When "yes" is always "yes" and "no" is always "no," when there is no apparent *difference* between the parents, the child is confronted with a stone wall. There is no way in which he can manoeuver, play one parent off against the other, exploit temporary divergences for his personal advantage. Mother and father tend to merge into one bland and adamant image, something not quite human and therefore deeply disturbing.

To observe people in conflict is a necessary part of a child's education. It helps him to understand and accept his own occasional hostilities and to realize that differing opinions need not imply an absence of love. One of my patients, a young woman of twenty-two, suffered from exaggerated feelings of guilt. She accused herself of malice and ingratitude toward her parents whom she presented as saint-like figures, literally too good to be true. There was a sudden and dramatic improvement in her condition when she discovered, through analysis, that they frequently quarreled. The quarrels always took place privately, behind the closed doors of their bedroom. As a young child, my patient had overheard some of these quarrels and been so upset by them that the parents took even greater care to conceal their differences. The relevant data came to light in the course of the analysis and was confirmed by the parents. A great load dropped from the young woman's mind. The revelation of their discord eased her guilt by giving her "permission" for her own discordant feelings.

I am not suggesting that parents make a practice of disagreeing in public nor that they seize every opportunity for airing resentment. But it is a mistake, where honest differences exist, to avoid their expression altogether. Such artificial harmony has a deadening effect; it tends to make timid conformists of the children, the kind of people who will give in to anything rather than risk an explosion. Better to have the sparks fly from time to time. They invigorate the atmosphere.

Among the precipitating causes of neuroses is one which, paradoxically, is more frequently found in the good home than the bad. That is the rivalry among brothers and sisters for the attention of their parents. Where the latter are harsh or indifferent, the siblings may band together for comfort, an excellent socializing influence in itself. Whether they do or not, however, they have little to gain from jealous competition. Loving parents, by contrast, are a prize worth fighting for and the struggle among the children may reach a pitch of real frenzy.

It is a thorny problem for the parents. The better they are, the more inordinate are the demands made upon them by their offspring. No matter how carefully they distribute their favors, how embracing their goodwill, they cannot entirely satisfy these demands. The children are like rival pretenders to a throne and their main object in life is to eliminate their competitors. Each child is determined to be the "only" child.

The rivalry expresses itself in various forms, according to the individual child's age, sex and temperament. Where circumstances seem feasible, actual physical assault may be employed. But there are other devices. Wheedling and excessive compliance pay off in increased attention. So does spectacular naughtiness. If everything else fails, there may be a resort to illness. The anxious solicitude of his parents, their concentration upon him, more than compensate the small invalid for the discomforts of fever, the pain of a sore throat.

Observers have often commented on the fact that the oldest child in a family is apt to be the most maladjusted. The usual explanation is that inexperienced parents are anxious parents, unduly concerned over the ordinary tribulations of infancy and with a tendency to panic when things go wrong. By the time other children appear, they have learned something about their job and treat it more calmly. The younger ones benefit from this change in attitude.

All this is undoubtedly true. But we should not ignore the significance of another factor. The oldest child is the only one who has ever enjoyed the exclusive affection of his parents, an enviable position. To him, it seems permanent and he is profoundly shocked when a rival suddenly appears upon the scene. An appreciable number of first-born children cannot forgive their par-

ents for the implied "rejection." The massive injury to
their self-esteem makes them sullen and resentful, hostile to their siblings, and forever unreconciled to the
injustice of their lot. For later children, who have been
forced to share attention from the beginning, the birth
of a new baby is never so deep a trauma. There was
always at least one serpent in their infantile paradise.
But we must remember that they, too, have had their
brief day as "crown prince" or "crown princess" of the
family, a role which no child cedes willingly. It probably contributes to the fierceness of sibling rivalry.

Most of the problems I have been discussing make
themselves felt during the very early stages of a child's
development. There are others whose significance is not
so immediately apparent but which, nevertheless, cause
undesirable tensions in otherwise happy homes. From
the parents' viewpoint, they are peculiarly slippery because so many of their own unconscious feelings are
involved. Buried feelings of this kind resist critical
appraisal.

There is, for instance, the question of money. "Good"
parents tend to be lavish with their children, materially
as well as emotionally. They spend on them all that
their means allow, and often more. But, while they
exert themselves to give their offspring the best of
everything—from toys to schools, and including orthodontia—there is a nagging worry in the background of
their minds. Are they, perhaps, spoiling the children?

Will they take their advantages for granted and never learn the true value of money? Or of anything else?

This anxiety, which is quite independent of financial status, and which sometimes covers up a much deeper one, may make the parents rather stingy at the most inappropriate times. Junior owns an English racing bicycle of the latest model but, if he wants to go to the movies with the other fellows, he has to touch Mother or Dad for the money. And Sister, who loves to shop at the dime store—picking out ribbons and belts and so forth, comparing prices and values, exercising her taste—is warned against extravagance. On the other hand, she has far more clothes than she needs and attends an expensive dancing-class.

No wonder that Junior and Sister are confused. No wonder if they begin to pocket any loose change they see lying around or even burrow surreptitiously in their mother's purse. The contradiction in the attitude of their parents does not escape them but they cannot understand it and it makes them resentful. It may also lead to irresponsibility in later life. They spend wildly then because they have not been trained to spend well, to balance what they want against their financial resources. Hard cash is unnecessary. With the magic phrase "Charge it," they summon up their parents and become dependent children again.

What prompts parents to so inconsistent a generosity? Why can't they see that they are defeating their own purposes? The problem, as I said before, is slippery.

Brought up themselves in a far less permissive environment, they may be protesting unconsciously against the
freedom they have given their children, the lack of
discipline, the easy talk about sex. They encourage it,
of course, since they want to be modern, but deep down
in their inhibited souls they shrink from such candor.
So they become mysterious and forbidding about money
instead. Authority makes its last stand on the financial
issue. Many children who know a lot about their parents' sexual relations are kept entirely ignorant of the
family budget.

There is another, even more insidious way in which
good parents may unconsciously put pressure on their
children. That is by being too good—so devoted and
self-sacrificing that their own existence becomes unduly
narrowed. They live not only *for* but *through* their
children, concentrating all their hopes upon these beloved surrogates in whom they have invested so much
of themselves. They may insist that they expect no return on the investment . . . that a child's life is his
own, etcetera etcetera. . . . They may even believe
that they mean what they say. If they do, they are de-
luding only themselves. Their children are not deluded.

A child from such a home realizes quite early that,
however strong they may seem otherwise, his parents
are vulnerable where he is concerned. When he is unhappy, they are unhappy; when he fails, they fail, too.
Though they are so good and kind and loving, they

are somehow a drag on him. He is uneasily aware that he is too much a part of them, or they of him; in any case, he cannot quite manage to be a separate person. As he gets older and understands what they have given up for his sake, this feeling is replaced by a sense of obligation. His identity is firmer but so is his conscience. He cannot break away from these two aging people who seem to have no life of their own; the very fact that he sometimes wants to makes him feel guilty, as ungrateful as the daughter who provoked Lear's anguished cry:

> "How sharper than a serpent's tooth it is
> To have a thankless child!"

The circumstances are different, of course, but anguish is anguish and he knows they are easily wounded, sensitive to the slightest hint of defection on his part. So he goes to a college near home instead of the one he had set his heart on and, later, he turns down an exciting job in South America. He may even hesitate to marry unless his choice is thoroughly approved. Unwittingly, animated only by the best intentions, his loving parents have produced a neurotic deformation in his character.

The process is not necessarily so drastic but parents of this kind are always a burden to the child. Their excessive devotion has given them a perpetual lien on his life; he has to carry the weight of their emotional needs in addition to his own. It may be more than he can bear and it is certainly more than he should be required to bear. His potentiality for happiness is diminished because they have staked their happiness in his. Any failure places him in double jeopardy. When disappointment is piled on disappointment and guilt added to the load, a minor set-back may drain away as much energy as a real but uncomplicated catastrophe.

Parents who martyr themselves for their children, without some concern for their own rights, some honest "selfishness," are neither effective people nor genuinely good parents. The unwritten charter of humanity has a clause which states: he who lives altogether for others betrays both himself and them.

One last point deserves a brief mention. In any home, good or bad, happy or unhappy, there is an unpredictable factor—the influences, outside the immediate family circle, to which the child is exposed and over which the parents have little or no control. No practicing psychiatrist can ignore these influences. As he is only too aware, many neuroses have their origin in traumatic experiences entirely unrelated to the family situation, unsuspected by the parents and frequently repressed by the child. A damaging experience of this kind may not be revealed, or even enter consciousness again, until many years later when the afflicted adult turns to analysis for help in his troubles.

One important "outside" influence, the earliest, is really "inside." It emanates from the many parental substitutes whom the child encounters in the form of hired help, neighbors, friends and relatives. Any one of these is potentially a Trojan horse within the citadel of the home. The more they are trusted, the greater is their capacity to harm.

This particular problem is most acute in the upper social brackets, where the children's care is delegated, as a matter of course, to people other than the parents. The traditional "Nannie" or "Mammy" had a powerful and not always wholesome influence on her charges but, in her case, there was at least some identification with the family she served and a high degree of personal loyalty. By adopting the family pattern as her own, she was able to transmit it to the children.

Such faithful retainers are seldom met with today. There is, instead, a fairly rapid turnover in the nurses, maids and governesses to whom the child is entrusted. He may become hopelessly confused by that constantly changing procession of guardians, insecure in his attachments and uncertain of his values. But that is not the only nor the most serious danger. With domestic help so hard to come by, standards of selection inevitably drop. Among that motley crew of parental substitutes are bound to be some misfits, unstable and even vicious personalities. The parents, eager to have "someone," are not disposed to be overly critical and often are compelled to make compromises. Such a situation is not apt to arise in the economically more modest home though an occasional baby-sitter, paid or voluntary, may cause trouble even there.

The emphasis—already great and still growing—on

group activities is taking children out of the home to a much larger extent than was formerly the case, and at an earlier age. They used to spend the pre-school years in the company of their parents and siblings exclusively. Now they trot, or rather toddle, to nurseries in the morning, join their playmates at supervised playgrounds in the afternoon and, altogether, have a rather full social life. At a slightly older age, they start going to camps during the summer vacations—a time of year once dedicated to family picnics. In fact, they are kept so busy "integrating with their contemporaries," under the direction of specially trained adults, that they have very little time to establish meaningful contacts with their natural parents. Parental influence thus becomes diluted while outside influences are correspondingly strengthened. Granted that most of them are healthy and productive; they cannot always be so, a fact which may account for otherwise inexplicable anomalies in the development of the child.

This is also true in the sexual sphere, where the parents' influence, even if reasonably good, may not be able to withstand that of contemporaries. A chance remark, overheard in the locker room at school, may have a much more lasting effect on the child's attitude than the elaborate explanations of his well-meaning parents. Too often, as Freud has pointed out, these are given him too late and "in mysterious and solemn language" from which he instinctively shrinks.

The mutual embarrassment attaching to sex is usually aggravated during adolescence when communication of any sort is exceedingly difficult. The typical adolescent is a bewildering mixture of traits, at once shy and assertive, desperately in need of guidance and resentful when it is offered. He tends to cover up the profound anxiety he feels with a know-it-all manner which is calculated to keep his parents at a distance. If they fall into the trap he has set for them, he becomes progressively alienated. That is why parents seldom know what happens to their children during this critical period. The traumatic experiences which may occur at camp, in boarding-school or during week-end visits are carefully concealed from them.

In discussing external influences, we cannot afford to neglect the impress on the community as a whole of parents who let their children run wild. Their over-permissiveness may stem from indifference or from their own neurotic confusion. Whatever the cause, they give their children complete latitude in such matters as staying out late, drinking, and using the family car whenever it suits them. Since these young people suffer none of the normal social restrictions, they are usually envied by their schoolmates who try to exact similar "freedoms" from their own families. They feel martyred by the prohibitions imposed on them and make unfavorable comparisons. The irresponsible parents are called "understanding" while the others come under the stigma of being impossibly old-fashioned.

Tremendous tensions develop under these circumstances. The struggle between the well-meaning parents and their importunate children may result in the disruption of hitherto good relationships. Even worse, the parents may weaken under the onslaught. Such an outcome is more likely if they are not too sure of themselves to begin with and if the offending family is prominent in the community. In the collapse of healthy standards, the rotten apple becomes the norm. We can sympathize with parents who are caught in this predicament but it is well to remind them that they will not purchase the affection of their children by retreating from their own honest beliefs. The doctrine of "peace at any price" is an invitation to further aggression. It has never yet won peace.

As I said before, there are no easy solutions. To bring up children, to turn these little savages into effective and reasonable adults, is a demanding occupation at best. In an age like ours, with its massive pressures and its constantly fluctuating values, the task may appear impossible. There is a despairing temptation to abandon the problem altogether or to deny its complexities by returning to an earlier and simpler approach. It is not only individuals who regress in the face of difficulties; a whole society may take this neurotic way out.

In reflecting on our paradox, one thing above all is worth emphasizing; happiness does not lead to unhappiness. When it seems to, there are other hidden factors

at work. It cannot be denied that the loving home—
where the parents are careful of each other's dignity and
the children, too, are regarded as people—sometimes
produces psychological casualties. For every such casu-
alty, however, there are literally thousands which are
the result of harshness or indifference in the family.

The odds are still on happiness. Let us not turn back.

CHAPTER 3

The Screaming Mother:

The Paradox of Emotional Control

"I can't take it any longer, Doctor. Maybe I was never meant to be a mother. I've done my best . . . I've tried to be patient, but he's too much for me. Johnny, I mean. I don't know how others do it. I can't take it. I'll go out of my mind if things keep on this way.

"It's this business of his not listening to me. I tell him the same thing over and over and over again, and it doesn't even seem to register with him. I know he's only five, but he's got to learn to listen.

"Just this morning, I kept asking him to play someplace else, not in the kitchen. First he almost tips over

*something on the stove . . . then he just stands in front
of the refrigerator letting all the cold air out . . . then
he makes a mess of the sink trying to wash dishes. I almost fell over him a couple of times with hot things in
my hands. He's got a room full of toys, and swings and
a sandbox outside. I tell him to go play with his friends,
but he hangs around doing things that needle me until
I just have to explode. When he spilled his milk all over
the floor today, I couldn't control myself any longer—
I screamed at him and hit him and his nose began to
bleed. I didn't mean to hit him that hard . . .*

*"Then I realized how unfair I was, that he's still a
baby and he doesn't mean to be bad. So I tried to make
it up to him. After he stopped crying, I took him out
for a soda and I spent the rest of the morning playing
with him. I told him I was sorry I hit him so hard, and
that I love him even when I get angry. I just let all my
work around the house go this morning because I felt
so bad.*

*"I want Johnny to grow up right. I'm so afraid,
though, if things go on this way, I'll make a mess of his
life."*

One could search through the manuals of child care
without finding an approving word for women like
Johnny's mother. She breaks all the rules, the careful
and reasonable guides for motherhood which it has
taken decades of laborious research to establish. From
the experts' point of view, she has never grown up her-

self and any children she may bear start out with a grave handicap. No doubt, she loves them but she cannot give them the calm and solid guidance they need for the difficult climb to maturity. With such a mother, they are bound to feel insecure.

The judgment seems plausible, especially when we remember how easy it is for a child to develop feelings of rejection. If, as I pointed out in the preceding chapter, he may misinterpret even the most loving attitudes, how can he fail to be damaged by such an open display of anger? How can he not be confused when authority is so fickle, when he is punished one minute and consoled the next?

But there is a paradox here: the children of these screaming mothers often turn out surprisingly well. Somehow or other, they manage to make the grade, to become happy and effective adults. And, on the other hand, I have seen some pretty poor specimens emerging from homes where the emotional barometer is always steady and both parents are models of self-control and understanding. That is not always or even usually the case but the paradox does obtain. I have covered some of the reasons for it in the chapter already mentioned. What I want to do now is to examine one particular aspect of this highly complex problem—the question of emotional control. If the screaming mother is sometimes, in defiance of the rules, an effective mother, we ought to know why.

It is not my intention to defend her, much maligned

as she is, nor to belittle the generally accepted theories about the best way to raise a child. The problem is similar, in certain respects, to the one I discussed in the first chapter of this book. Just as no wedded couple has ever been able to meet the "average" standards of the marriage manuals, so can no woman completely live up to the rules which manuals on successful parenthood recommend to their readers. Reasonable as most of them are, they should be taken with the proverbial grain of salt. The ideal mother, like the ideal marriage, is a fiction.

Emotional control is so emphasized in the manuals that their lack of it makes many conscientious women feel wholly inadequate. Troubled patients cite this one fault as glaring evidence of their unfitness for motherhood, an opinion often shared by their husbands. "Why does she have to be so emotional? She's ruining the children," is a common complaint. Justified or not, it merely compounds the poor woman's difficulties. And it is rarely justified.

Before we go any further, it would be well to make one point clear. Much of the censure attaching to the uncontrolled, emotionally volatile mother is based on an unwarranted comparison of her behavior with that of the psychotic mother. The latter is profoundly disorientated, mentally and emotionally at sea. She rages and rants and punishes her children for reasons which have nothing to do with them and which literally "make no sense" from any normal point of view.

The "screaming mother" I am concerned with in this discussion is another sort of person altogether. She makes a lot of sense. Her impulses are healthy and so are her responses; they are directly and meaningfully related to the external situation. In other words, to her children. Her trouble is that there is no delayed action fuse in her temperamental equipment. She reacts quickly and, when the reaction is one of anger, she screams. But she is just as ready to express tenderness or gaiety or remorse. However volatile her feelings may be, they always find an appropriate physical outlet.

That spontaneity is one of her greatest assets as a mother. The language of the emotions is unmistakable; it leaves no room for doubt. There is no other way of establishing contact with the infant and it remains the most vital channel of communication throughout the child's formative years. Almost primitive in its simplicity and directness, it is a language which the woman who reins herself in too much is apt to forget. Unwilling to respond negatively, she may lose the ability to respond positively as well. By the mere fact of continually stopping to think, she erects a mental barrier and such barriers are notoriously hard to break down.

Inhibitions of this kind are refreshingly absent in the screaming mother. She is unable or unwilling to stop and think and she wears no mask. What she feels, what she is, are plain as day, an enormous advantage to the child. There is no need to wonder, no possible chance for misinterpretation. She is a primer of the emotions and he can read her without effort.

Emotional reactions are deeply rooted in the personality; unlike intellectual attitudes, they are not subject to change without notice. Because the uninhibited mother expresses *herself,* her actual feelings rather than those she thinks she ought to feel, her impact upon her children is relatively consistent. From day to day, month to month, year to year, she remains the same woman. Early in life, they find out just what makes her happy or sad and what actions of theirs provoke her to fury. Her moods may veer as erratically as the wind but the emotional climate she creates is thoroughly predictable. That, too, is a priceless boon to the developing child. His mother's consistency as a person clarifies his relations with her. It lets him know where he stands.

Does it seem odd and paradoxical to pin the label of consistency on such a highly volatile creature? Only if we confuse the emotional with the irrational. There is a reason for her moods. The needle of a sensitive instrument is also wildly agitated. But it moves in response to shifting factors in the environment and it registers them accurately. The criteria by which we measure emotional health are not nearly as consistent as the untutored responses of these overly reactive women.

When we are dealing with a basic relationship, deliberate intellectual constructions may become cumbersome. Put into practice, they often disturb a balance which involves factors not yet known or completely understood. The relationship between mother and child, in its early stages anyway, is not so much illogical as non-logical. It is mediated through emotional channels which, in the broad sense, vary very little, if at all, from one generation to another. Nevertheless, each mother and child constitute an individual entity; they have to feel each other out as though there were no precedent for their own particular bond.

It is obvious that we cannot ask the mother to rely too much on theories. On the one hand, they are too variable, influenced by the times in which they originate, changing their content and emphasis to accord not only with newly-discovered facts but with prevailing social ideals. On the other, being abstractions, they are not flexible enough to cover every individual situation. That is why the admirably-controlled modern mother, who brings up her child by the book, may go so very far wrong. She lets logic take the place of instinct, reason of emotion. Between her and the child she has brought into the world the lines of communication are clogged.

The screaming mother is incapable of that heroic detachment and thus she never fails to make emotional contact with her child. Kindred souls, they react upon each other continually, a healthy give-and-take which is probably the most significant of all experiences for the developing child. This mutual responsiveness sets the pattern for all his future relationships. It protects him against the sense of aloneness, of isolation from his kind, which motivates the tortured withdrawal of the schizophrenic. It makes him feel real, a living, kicking, screaming somebody who proves his existence by the very fact that he can make an observable impression with his antics, evoke an intelligible response. The smooth mask of the controlled mother, her invincible calm, may be very disturbing to the infant who is engaged in the process of establishing an identity.

At the risk of redundance, I must emphasize again the fundamental importance to the child of not feeling emotionally isolated. The sense of "togetherness" overrides all other considerations in the parent-child relationship. In the analysis of both children and adults, we constantly find evidence that there is a basic affectionate bond with the responsive parent, even though the response may at times be negative. By contrast, no amount of kindness and devotion will make up for the absence of such emotional interplay. It is paradoxical how often the screaming parent is feared and resented less than the controlled and kindly one.

But let us return to the screaming mother. There is another way in which, by simply being her volatile self, she serves her child well. Like the coach in an academy of the dramatic arts, she shows him how emotions are expressed. Her spontaneous outbursts, as well as the rich diversity of her reactions, make her a wonderful object for study and mimicry. The child learns both by watching and by having to react in his turn. A whole

wordless vocabulary is transmitted to him through his
mother's touch, her gestures, the varying tones of her
voice, all the movements of her body. He discovers the
difference in meaning between a slap and a caress, between the head tossed back in anger and that same head
bent over him in pity and gentleness.

Such training in emotional expression—which, to be
successful, must take place in the earliest formative
years—is of the utmost importance to the child. Having,
as it were, "rehearsed" his feelings in the protected atmosphere of the home, he is prepared for performance
on a larger stage. Emotionally competent, he is able to
convey what he feels to others and to judge, with a reasonable degree of accuracy, their reactions to him. This
acuity is a valuable tool when he begins to consort with
his contemporaries. Children tend to make contact, as
animals do, through non-verbal processes. They sniff,
they circle, they stretch out a tentative paw. Having
taken each other's measure, their decision is apt to be
final, not subject to argument. In this uncovenanted society of the young, outcasts are recognized at a glance
and often ruthlessly treated.

The youngsters so marked—usually those who have
been deprived of the basic emotional training—may
withdraw in alarm from their ferocious contemporaries
and seek refuge among the elders to whom they have
become accustomed. But, to be acceptable, they must
ingratiate themselves, truckle under, be wholly sub-
servient to their adult protectors. Ladies and gentlemen

before their time, they forfeit their position in the democracy of childhood, missing out on its pleasures as well as on its unique educational opportunities. These "perfect" children, so docile and well-mannered, so pleasing to their parents, may shock us severely later in life. Without warning, without apparent cause, they go into a tailspin. Their outraged impulses have exacted a fitting revenge.

It is fortunate that most mothers are not as "good" mothers as they would like to be, not as calm and controlled and super-human. Because they are not, the majority of children manage to acquire the rudiments of emotional expression and get along fairly well with others of their age. Their difficulties, as a general rule, are not with their contemporaries but with their parents.

Take the normal problems of discipline. In the average modern home, they may become the source of incredible confusion, with parents and children facing each other across a gulf of misunderstanding. Here, again, the screaming mother, in spite or because of her temperamental traits, has certain specific advantages. No child of hers is ever in doubt over what she would like or not like him to do. He knows because she lets him know—immediately, within a split second. She does not wait to decide whether the prohibited act justifies punishment or to strike the correct disciplinary attitude. Without consulting the book or even her own conscience, without taking time to discuss the matter

with her husband or her psychiatrist, she reacts to the
situation at hand. It is quite possible that she may react
too harshly but her severity is redeemed by its prompt-
ness. When punishment follows crime so instanta-
neously, the child has a clear conception of the kind
of behavior it would be wise to avoid in the future.
Thinking out the disciplinary act, as the over-con-
scientious mother is moved to do, fuzzes the issue. By
the time punishment is inflicted, the child may have
forgotten the nature of his offense. As far as he is concerned, it is probably not an offense anyway. The world
of adult values is in large part inexplicable to him, and
entirely arbitrary. He conforms with it only because
he has to.

That is why it is difficult to reason with a very young
child, as so many well-meaning mothers are tempted
to do. They are appealing to a faculty which has not
yet developed and their efforts are doomed to frustration. When a carefully modulated voice explains to the
child the virtues of cleanliness, or discourses at length
on the beauty of the vase he has smashed, it might just
as well be discussing the quantum theory. Nor is he enlightened by a commentary on the perils of playing with
matches or rushing out into the midst of traffic. The
only peril he recognizes is the loss of love and the only
social pressure he responds to is the approval or disapproval of his parents. This must be communicated to
him in terms he can understand, emotional terms.
Otherwise, he becomes troubled and confused, ob-

scurely aware that something is expected of him but not
at all sure what that something is. What does convey
itself to him is that he may very well be in danger of dis-
pleasing this incomprehensible creature who holds his
fate in her hands. Calculated intellectual appeals, if per-
sisted in, add up to a rather cruel kind of manipulation
—cruel because they subtly undermine the child's sense
of security.

The screaming mother is temperamentally incapable
of such manipulation. It does not occur to her to argue
with the child and she does not delude either herself
or him with the idea that he is doing what *he* wants to
do when it is *she* who wants him to do it. She simply
explodes when things go wrong, a gratifyingly clear indication of her wishes and a warning of what will happen if they are again disregarded.

This same trigger-quick temperament makes it impossible for her to be over-permissive. She has not the
patience for it and thus most of the problems which I
discussed in the last chapter do not arise for her at all.
None of that nonsense about equal rights, no bogus
democracy for this mother. When the need arises, she
makes no bones about exercising her authority. Her
children may resent her dominance but they do not
question it; the facts are too plain. Both parties are
spared the agonizing and inconclusive tug-of-war which
takes place when mothers want their children to behave
in a certain fashion but hesitate to impose their wills
too openly for fear of seeming tyrannical. When au-

thority is so reluctant, the setting-up of satisfactory behavior patterns becomes a matter of chance. It all depends on who can hold out longer—the little savage or
the civilizing agent, his mother. Moreover, whatever the
outcome, the child remains fundamentally undisciplined; since he receives no direct orders, but is instead
seduced or tricked into compliance, he does not know
how to obey. That ignorance unfits him for the larger
world he must some day enter. Besides damaging his
capacity to form a strong conscience, it may result in
specific traumas.

Dramatic evidence of the way in which roundabout
disciplinary methods may boomerang was recently
brought to me by one of my patients. The subject was
her little boy whom she had treated with exaggerated
care from the time of his birth. A former social worker,
she had absorbed all the prevailing theories; she was
convinced that one must never browbeat a child or ex-
pose him to emotional storms. She had also convinced
her husband. Both of them leaned over backwards
fantastically in their behavior with the child. They took
great pains to avoid using negative terms when he had
to be prevented from doing something. They even made
it a practice to lean down when addressing him so that
he would not be overwhelmed by their superior height.

The word "don't" was never used to the child. If, for
instance, he tried to touch a hot stove, his mother would
distract him from his efforts in an elaborate and ingenious fashion, not only engaging his attention else-

where but giving him a positive compensation in the form of amusement. In keeping with this circuitous technique, she made complicated arrangements when the boy's younger brother was born to dissipate any possible feelings of rejection or sibling rivalry.

The boy throve and the parents congratulated themselves. Everything was fine until his first day at school. He stood around in the schoolyard with the other novices, curious, expectant and seemingly quite unafraid. A teacher came up and told the children to form a line, preparatory to entering the classroom. About half of them obediently fell into place. The others, including this child, dawdled. The teacher repeated the order, raising her voice to the proper authoritarian pitch. The laggards responded promptly, with the single exception one might anticipate. At this point he began to vomit and had to be sent home. It was three weeks before he was well enough to return.

What happened? Why did this child react so violently to the teacher's instructions? Well, emotionally, he had been wrapped in cotton-wool all his life. Unlike the other children, he had never been spoken to sharply. It was, for him, a new and frightening experience, something he was completely unprepared for. In his own family, his own home, the voice of authority was absent. To hear it for the first time in such unfamiliar circumstances proved a major shock.

It is possible, too, that the boy was reacting to a sudden uprush of anger in himself for which the vomiting served as outlet—an anger directed, incidentally, not at the teacher but at his mother. She had, in effect, pushed him out of the cosy nest where he had always been so comfortable and placed him in a terrifying situation. His perhaps unrealized resentment over being sent to school—sent *away,* in the interpretation of many children—then broke through in a violently symbolical act. He spewed forth his rage and, simultaneously, rejected the mother who had rejected him. A child brought up as he was would not be able to express resentments more directly. The extraordinary manipulative techniques to which he had been subjected probably blocked them from entering consciousness at all.

The repression of hostility may create a host of problems in homes, like that of my patient, which put a premium on emotional control. Hostility is, after all, one of the basic drives in any personality and it cannot simply be wished out of existence. Every human being has aggressive impulses; there is no intimate relationship in which they do not play a part. That is as true of the parent-child relationship as of any other. Perhaps more so, since it involves such profound conflicts of interest, so many sacrifices on both sides.

Many troubles would be avoided if one fact were admitted from the outset: it is impossible for any woman to love her children twenty-four hours a day. Unfortunately, many good women feel it is incumbent on them to maintain this fiction. They stifle their quite natural irritation, concealing it very often not only from the children but even from themselves. If it does rise to consciousness, they are overwhelmed by feelings of guilt.

We frequently observe this guilt reaction in the immediate post-partum period. The normal woman looks forward to the birth of her child. While she may have some fears connected with the delivery itself, she expects that all will be well once the child is in her arms. After the months of waiting and dreaming, she is prepared for a great surge of love.

It doesn't always work out that way. The circumstances of the birth—the combination of anesthesia, loss of blood and shock—may prove too much for her. Unacknowledged resentments swarm to the very threshold of her consciousness, inducing a mood of panicky withdrawal. Presented with her baby, she feels strange and numb, unaccountably alienated from the odd little creature who has become her responsibility, whom she must watch and feed and care for in the months and years to come.

It is not unnatural to shrink from this responsibility. The very young baby, especially, is more of a chore than a joy; it has little to offer, in the way of affectionate response, in return for the trouble it causes. But many new mothers are horrified by what seems to them a lack of maternal feeling. They should not, they believe, even be thinking of such things. The mild depression so often encountered among them expresses their sense of guilt.

As a rule, it vanishes when they recover their

strength. They find that their duties, though onerous, are not beyond their capacities. A sense of pride, the concomitant of creative action, restores their psychic energy and helps them to deal with the passing irritations which again arouse ambivalent feelings. These are to be expected during practically every stage of the mother-child relationship. As I said before, the mother is the civilizing agent; her task, in many ways a thankless one, is to transform a spewing, incontinent, irrational and often intractable young animal into what is at least the approximation of a social being. To assume that this can be done without resentments on both sides is wishful thinking.

The woman who cannot admit that she sometimes feels angry with her children, who hides every aggressive impulse behind a façade of angelic patience, is not doing them a favor. Her repressed hostility may be turned against her husband, a luckless servant or some other adult in the environment, embittering the atmosphere of the home. Worst of all, it may be turned against herself. The guilt so engendered is a slow but deadly poison which cannot fail to affect her personality. She is constantly on guard, afraid to relax her control even for a moment. All her energies may become engaged in this unproductive effort, making her dull and unresponsive emotionally, as incapable of genuine affection as she is of rage. Like an automaton, she goes through the motions of loving, but her children feel no warmth. Aware of her failure to relate to them adequately, her lack of true "motherliness," her guilt increases. So do her tensions. They may rise to such a pitch that, to prevent an explosion, she has to send the children away from home prematurely—to nurseries, camps and boarding-schools. Freed of their disturbing presence, she can love them as she thinks she should, without hostility. It is only, ironically, by abdicating her responsibilities that she can again become the "ideal" mother of the manuals.

Such a grotesque travesty of motherhood is fortunately beyond the reach of the over-reacting and demonstrative woman. She holds back nothing; she cannot. It is impossible for her resentments to pile up inside her and form an emotional barrier between her and her children. They spend themselves as they arise, in relatively harmless outbursts which clear the air like a summer storm. Once over, the sun comes out again as warm as before. Her love is not clouded by unexpressed resentments.

Neither is her children's. Earlier in this chapter, I discussed how important it is for their development to learn how to recognize and reveal their own emotions. That is particularly true where antagonisms are concerned. The child must be taught how to handle them early in life if he is to function with assurance in a competitive and conflict-ridden world. Self-assertion is a valuable tool and so, at certain times, is the capacity

for anger. There are times when people have to be re-
sisted and situations corrected. In a meaningful life,
rejection plays as vital a role as acceptance.

Aggressive impulses should not be denied or suppressed but *educated*—as they are when the normal
tensions between parent and child find adequate expression. In these miniature battles, the child tests his
strength and resourcefulness and, simultaneously, discovers the limits of tolerable behavior. That is excellent
training. But he cannot get it if his mother refuses to
join in the fray; the woman who always keeps herself
under strict control cheats her child of his first and
most necessary foil. Lacking a responsive object, he is
unable to exercise his anger effectively. It becomes
blunted against his mother's unyielding calm or shat-
ters itself in an impotent temper tantrum. Such tantrums are a symptom of overwhelming frustration, a
warning that the child's aggressiveness is completely out
of hand. Like the savage who runs amok, he has murder
in his heart but he is both too bewildered and too helpless to carry out his intentions. The tantrum is, in a
sense, a plea for aid against an impulse which has become self-destructive.

Rage in itself is normal enough, an inevitable component of the civilizing process. No child likes to be
thwarted, as he must be to some extent even in the
most permissive homes. The curious thing is that children from such homes sometimes hate their parents
with a really extraordinary intensity. It is possible that,

being so much indulged, their tolerance to any kind of discipline is low. Or that they interpret the careful manipulation to which they are subjected as evidence of an essential coldness to themselves, equating controlled behavior with a lack of love. We cannot rule out these explanations. But it is also possible that overly solicitous parents put too great a burden on the conscience of their children, who are hard put to justify their resentment toward these good and kind and patient people. It seems wrong and yet there it is, a fact. Without quite knowing why, they feel intolerably guilty.

Rage and guilt combined make a brew which no child can assimilate without harm to himself. As he grows older, he may come to loathe everything connected with his early environment, making absurd charges against his parents, the rage and the guilt reinforcing each other and, incidentally, tearing him into shreds. Or his fury may turn wholly inwards, all self-esteem vanishing under that amorphous but pervasive sense of guilt. He becomes increasingly dependent and submissive because he does not dare to be himself.

The screaming mother, by virtue of her very faults, drives her children's resentments into the open. The anger she so frequently displays justifies their anger, leaving very little room for remorse. No matter how hateful they are, how naughty and rebellious, she provides them with a ready-made excuse for their behavior. To be able to rationalize aggression in this way is a great comfort. It lightens appreciably the load of guilt which we are all compelled to carry with us into maturity.

Unresolved aggressions are not, of course, the only source of guilt, nor perhaps the most important. Very early in life, a crust of culpability becomes attached to the sexual impulses, largely but not altogether as the result of wounds received in training. Speaking realistically, it is almost impossible to bring up a child in our society without in some way disturbing him sexually. A totally restrictive attitude—the kind we associate with the word "Victorian"—is almost certain to crush the child's capacity to make a healthy and mature adjustment to the sexual mores of today. We are not living in Samoa, however, and undue permissiveness may prove equally damaging, though in a different way. The intelligent parent, in approaching the problem, would obviously look for a middle ground between the two extremes. But that middle ground, unfortunately, is a very large area in which there are only a few signposts and those not too clearly marked. It has become apparent in recent years that, in handling the sexual impulses and curiosities of the child, no single method can be guaranteed to work in all cases. There are too many imponderables, both social and individual, to be taken into account.

That being so, every mother has to grope her way among conflicting standards. But, unless she is excessively swayed by purely intellectual formulas, her approach to the problem will necessarily be in terms of her own background, her own fears, the cultural milieu in which she lives and the sexual adaptation she herself has made. If she adheres steadfastly to what she genuinely believes is right, and is not completely out of tune with her environment, any mistakes she may make will not be too serious. In no other aspect of a child's training do consistency and sincerity count for so much.

It is not easy for modern parents to be emotionally honest about sex. Having convinced themselves that all its early manifestations are natural and healthy, they insist upon being tolerant, far more tolerant very often than in fact they are. They encourage their child to ask questions and they refuse to be shocked by anything he says or does. Or, anyway, to reveal their shock. They are determined to spare this little innocent of theirs the needless and agonizing inhibitions which were a consequence of their own much stricter upbringing. He is not going to be made to feel ashamed of anything connected with his body or its functions. Not if they can help it.

Well, nine times out of ten, they can't help it. Advanced theories trip up against unconscious obstacles. The child reacts, as he always does, not to what they say but to what they feel. He is quick to notice their averted eyes, the embarrassment which tightens their voices. Inevitably, he becomes both confused and distrustful and, after a while, embarrassed himself. Later

on, he will close his ears to the well-meaning little
"lectures" they prepare for his edification, uncom-
fortably aware that his parents do not really practice
what they preach and, at the same time, unable to
charge them with deception. A pattern of mutual hypoc-
risy is initiated which may lead to a profound alienation. The wry comment which Freud made on this
subject almost fifty years ago is, regrettably, still valid today: "Most of the answers to the question 'How can I
tell my children?' make such a pitiful impression . . .
that I should prefer parents not to concern themselves
with the explanation at all." *

The screaming mother may not contribute much to
her child's sexual enlightenment but, in this field as in
others, her candid reactions are of considerable value.
While her attitude may be wrong—repressive or foolishly over-excited—it is not dishonest; it reflects what
she really feels. It is not inconsistent, either; she could
not, if she would, adapt her behavior to the shifting
theories of the experts. She presents her child with a
set of values which are rooted in her personality and
which become, through his long and intimate contact
with her, unconsciously rooted in his. More often than
not, these values are part of a social pattern so that the
child is in tune with the group among which he moves,
never isolated, never alien. He may reject the pattern

* Sigmund Freud, "The Sexual Enlightenment of Children," Collected Papers, Vol. II. London, The Hogarth Press, 1924.

later, when he is himself adult, but he is always sustained by its emotional solidity.

If I have concentrated exclusively on the assets of the screaming mother, it is not because I wish to minimize her liabilities. They are many and as obvious to her children as they are to everybody else. Her virtues, on the other hand, are seldom recognized. They deserve some stress and not for her sake alone. We need an antidote to the over-rational approach which is nowadays so prevalent among conscientious parents. Emotional control is an excellent thing but we have made too much of it if we sacrifice, in its name, the far greater excellence of emotional rapport. When that is lacking between parents and children, the latter become psychically orphaned and the home a kind of institution.

Bringing up a family should be an adventure, not an anxious discipline in which everybody is constantly graded for performance. Many parents fail simply because they try too hard. They worry themselves and poke and prod their offspring—as though, by taking thought, they might somehow produce the "perfect" child, a paragon conforming in every respect to the standards of adjustment set up by the manuals. In the end, their children turn out no better than others who have not been so carefully cultivated and, sometimes, they turn out worse.

It is a paradoxical fact that some of the saddest, most

difficult youngsters come from homes which are theoretically ideal, where the parents are marvels of understanding and patience, like the ones I described earlier in this chapter. They loved their little boy and they wanted to give him a good start in life. But, in the process, they created a make-believe world and deprived him of themselves, the real father and mother from whom he could have learned so much. He never understood them and so he could not relate to them emotionally and find out from them what people are like.

By comparison, the young Johnny of our prologue had a splendid education. His mother was not a figment, the self-created image of the ideal mother, but a real person, fallible, tempestuous and thoroughly human. She let him see just what made her tick—she couldn't help it!—and he was beginning to learn how to handle her, a psychic acquisition of tremendous value. Indoctrinated as Johnny was in the rough and tumble of existence, it is unlikely that he would be daunted by any later experiences.

It is not enough for parents to understand children. They must accord children the privilege of understanding them.

CHAPTER 4

Great Expectations:

The Paradox of the Beautiful Woman

Was this the face that launched a thousand ships
And burnt the topless towers of Ilium?
Sweet Helen, make me immortal with a kiss (Kisses her)
Her lips suck forth my soul; see where it flies!

In what was perhaps his last discussion of the subject, Freud suggested that we turn to the poets if we want to know more about femininity. It is true that these few lines from Marlowe's "Dr. Faustus" tell us more about men than about women. They do, however, give a clue to one of the strangest paradoxes of psychology—

the fact that beautiful women find it harder than most others to achieve a satisfying sexual and emotional relationship.

Helen of Troy, with her supreme and fateful beauty, has always been the legendary symbol of such women, and for good reason. Her history is illuminating. Unhappily married to the rather uncouth Menelaus—substitute any self-made captain of industry—she was seduced and carried off by a charming sophisticated bounder. (There had been a similar incident in her early youth, from which she was rescued by her brothers.) Her life with Paris was unsatisfactory from the beginning and he soon neglected her. Meanwhile, her husband and the other Greek chieftains used her abduction as a pretext for making war on Troy. Her lover was killed in the course of the ten-year struggle and she drifted into a brief liaison with his brother. But, when the Greeks triumphed, she let them take her home. She was still an extraordinarily beautiful woman but it is probable that nothing much mattered to her at this point. In any case, she was accustomed to being the prize.

She remained a prize even after her death. Her weary ghost was summoned from the shades by the devil, in part payment of his bargain with Faustus. From the latter, she had to listen to all the usual nonsense, paeans to her beauty mixed with ill-disguised reproaches. Certainly, as his words to her prove, he was no better a lover than the others.

What is Faustus really saying to Helen in the lines I have quoted? Let us analyze them as well as we can. He is irrationally exalted, of course, as men are apt to be in the presence of feminine beauty, but his meaning is clear enough. In the first two, he holds her actively responsible for the Trojan war, a charge which ignores the facts but permits him to over-estimate her power for purposes of his own. He reveals them in the next line, where he asks her for something which is manifestly impossible. It is an infantile demand, clothing a fantastic wish in socially acceptable language. (But, then, Faustus has always indulged in magical thinking, anyway.) The fourth line gives him away completely. Having kissed her, he becomes frightened by the intensity of his feeling. And so he accuses her, in effect, of making him impotent.

Reduced to these matter-of-fact terms, the passage expresses very well what the beautiful woman is up against in her relations with men. Nevertheless, while she cannot be blamed for their phantasies about her—I shall go into the motivation of these later—there is no doubt that she often aggravates an already difficult situation by emotional attitudes as unrealistic as theirs. She is, in a sense, smitten by her own beauty and the phantasies it nourishes in her collide head-on with those it has awakened in the man. The outcome cannot be happy. It is sometimes disastrous.

No wonder that history and literature sound such a tragic note when they recount the stories of beautiful women. They wind before us in a sorrowful procession, enchanting and enchanted, lovely lost creatures with doom on their lips and in their eyes. They did not know they were doomed, they expected something quite different, the rare and shining destiny which nature reserves for her darlings. The trouble is that their assumption was false; they are not nature's darlings. Outstanding beauty, like outstanding gifts of any kind, tends to get in the way of normal emotional development, and thus of that particular success in life which we call happiness.

The classic heroines who do wind up happy ever after are cut to a different pattern. Their expectations are modest—the love of one good man is about all they dare to hope for—and their beauty, if they have it, is not intimidating but as shy and unemphatic as they are. As a matter of fact, it rarely blossoms until the hero comes around, a circumstance very gratifying to his ego and auspicious as far as their future relations are concerned. This flower he has discovered is his alone; there are no rivals in the offing and, should any show up, he can count on her not to pay any attention to them.

Women of this kind pose no threat to men. It is otherwise with the Helens, the Iseults and the Guineveres. They are, quite literally, "stunning"; their beauty strikes like lightning and may be equally dangerous. The man is rash who believes he can possess them and still live as other men live.

It is true that these women belong to fiction or, rather, to that curious dream-soaked world which lies halfway between fiction and unrecorded history. But they are still representative. Long before individual poets interpreted their stories, they had been worked over by the phantasy of anonymous generations of men. That is what makes them so true psychologically. All we have to do is strip off the romantic trappings, a defense against insights too painful to be borne. Women like those dim romantic heroines are around us today. They are just as much of a problem to themselves and to the men whom their beauty attracts.

The problem was dramatized for me one afternoon when an exceedingly lovely woman showed up for her first appointment. Her beauty was of the kind which permits no argument; it was simply there. And though, as she told me later, she was forty years old, she was as sensuously provocative as it is possible for a woman to be. Yet the first thing she said, to my surprise, was this: "Doctor, aren't there any potent men left in the world?"

Her story was sad, and there was a shabbiness about it, a feeling that the same blunders had been repeated too often, that under the fine clothes and the smooth unlined skin she was somehow in tatters. She had had three marriages and innumerable affairs. Her third marriage, which had taken place only three years before, was on the point of breaking up. She felt desperate about it and was developing marked hypochondriacal symptoms. Though she had shown no signs of it yet, she spoke with terror of her approaching menopause.

Sexual difficulties were responsible for wrecking both her marriages and her love affairs. They were not, she claimed, her fault. She was "always" ready for the sex act, enjoyed it and occasionally reached orgasm. The trouble, according to her, stemmed from her husbands and lovers. With monotonous regularity and in a short space of time, they all developed such failings as loss of erection or premature ejaculation. That was the reason, she said, for her opening question to me.

It was obvious that this woman "did something" to men, afflicting them with a radical sense of insecurity. Her attitude was a very arrogant one. Implicit in it was a challenge: "Let's see what you can do. Everybody else has failed me." Any man who came into contact with her sexually was placed in a kind of test situation which promptly precipitated anxiety on his part and a consequent loss of healthy sexual reflexes.

She had not always been so arrogant, however. At the time of her first marriage, she was only nineteen, a virgin and, from what I was able to gather, sexually receptive. She had, of course, been much courted and there had been a good deal of petting and necking during her adolescence. But she had frankly preferred the man who became her husband and she remained faithful to him as long as the marriage lasted. Nevertheless, he became increasingly jealous, resenting the attentions paid her by other men. As his potency waned, he began to accuse her of deliberately egging them on and became obsessed with the idea of her possible infidelity. The strain was too great. At the end of three years, they separated.

She did not marry again until the age of twenty-eight, a marriage which lasted a brief two years. Before it was over, she again embarked on the sexual adventures which had occupied her in the intervening years. Apparently, she had no trouble in finding partners; men pursued her wherever she was. But, as time went on, only the more aggressive type of male approached her, and every one of them felt obliged to compare his performance with that of her previous lovers. She had become, as it were, a touchstone of potency. Not unnaturally, these relationships came to grief. Of them all, only one was genuinely satisfactory, a liaison with a married man which began when she was thirty-three. There was no arrogance in her manner when she spoke of him and she said, rather pathetically, that she still loved him. But he had shown no desire to break up his marriage for her sake. When he called her, as he did occasionally even now, he treated her with polite gallantry. Unlike her other lovers, he evidently possessed a strong instinct for self-preservation.

My patient had borne two children, one each to her first two husbands. They had not helped, in any way, to cement the marriages nor to mitigate the hostility with which these men subsequently regarded her. She herself loved the children and had tried, in her way, to be a conscientious mother—that is, when the effort did not intrude too much on her main occupation, the frantic search for personal fulfillment.

What can we learn from this lovely and distraught woman? Well, for one thing, that great physical beauty may, in itself, be a castrating influence. Analytic literature is filled with examples of castrating women but, to my knowledge, passive beauty as such has never been regarded in that light. The reason no doubt, is that, by the time the beautiful woman is studied analytically, she is already frustrated and bitter and, consciously or unconsciously, hostile to men.

What happened to my patient in her first marriage is indicative of the point I want to make. She was not hostile then but an eager young girl, glowing with life and hope and the desire for happiness. She had found her dream prince, she had picked him out from a host of suitors—proof enough, one would think, that she cared for him above all others, that it was he who answered her need. She had given further proof by bearing his child. But, though he seemed to be an otherwise normal young man, he could not accept her reassurance. He was jealous, suspicious and, finally, impotent. Why?

I have spoken, in an earlier chapter, of the residual insecurity felt by most men in our civilization with regard to their sexual prowess. This is enormously intensified when the girl a man falls in love with is one of those ravishing beauties who attract swarms of admirers. Their mere presence may reawaken early anxieties; it throws him back into the typical competitive situation of adolescence where father, older brothers and more experienced contemporaries are all regarded as rivals. No matter how much the girl may seem to favor him, he cannot forget that there are other choices open to her, that he is, in a very real sense, surrounded by enemies who may, at any moment, snatch his prize away. Marriage does not solve his problem. Unless he takes his bride to a desert island, he cannot escape the threatening wolves. So he watches apprehensively for omens of disaster, misinterpreting the most casual glances or gestures. To his wife it sometimes seems that he *wants* to be convinced of her infidelity. She is probably right.

The truth is that marriage to a beautiful woman may rouse in the man fears far more deeply buried than the ones I have just described. For the latter, there is some realistic sanction, however slight. These others are pure phantasy. They mark the revival of a cluster of infantile emotions so thoroughly repressed that they are usually inaccessible to consciousness.

Let us assume that, for the briefest of moments, they do become conscious. What happens? Something quite absurd, and yet devastating in its impact. The adult male looks at the lovely young girl and sees his mother.

Not his real mother, of course, not the aging woman whom he regards with tolerant affection and whose cheek he probably pecked as he started out for the party. What he sees is the heroine of the first great drama of his life, the oedipal mother, a being so infinitely desirable that any woman he may subsequently love is no more than the shadow of that radiant image. She may have been, objectively considered, a very ugly woman— pock-marked, deformed, with straggling greasy hair. That is of no importance. It was the magnitude of his need that made her beautiful, that indeed engendered in him the very idea of beauty.

This forbidden mother-image lurks in the heart of every man who has not been totally rejected or psychotically arrested in his development and affects, to a greater or less extent, all his relations with women. That is why, as Freud has said, ". . . whoever is to be really free and happy in love must have overcome his deference for women and come to terms with the idea of incest." * There is no doubt, however, that the beautiful woman —by the mere fact of being beautiful—reactivates that image almost automatically. The taboos with which it is associated are unconsciously transferred to her, making her at once more desirable—since what is forbidden or unavailable is what we long for most—and more frightening than ordinary women are. Shrouded in a mysterious aura of dread and delight, she becomes the acme of femininity, Woman herself.

She becomes even more. By the logic of the unconscious mind, which indiscriminately fuses all repressed material, the beautiful woman also inherits the attri-

* Sigmund Freud, "The Most Prevalent Form of Degradation in Erotic Life," Collected Papers, Volume IV. London, The Hogarth Press, 1925.

butes of an earlier and far more awe-inspiring figure, the pre-oedipal or phallic mother. Like some ancient deities, she has both male and female characteristics and, to childish eyes, her power seems absolute. All-loving, she is capable of anger; what she gives so lavishly, she can always take away again. To displease her is to risk much—not only the withdrawal of her love and protection but another punishment too dreadful to contemplate. What punishment? Little boys know the answer. It is the loss or immobilization of that incomparable organ which is their greatest treasure, without which they would not be little boys at all.

By the time he enters the oedipal period, the boy knows the difference between male and female. The Great Mother is only a woman now. He loves her but it is his father, normally, of whom he is in awe. His consuming ambition to possess the now wholly feminine parent runs up against the prior rights exercised by this strong and admirable male in whose good graces he must, at all costs, remain. Reluctantly, and not always decisively, the boy renounces his ambition. The parental "no" becomes internalized, an edict of his own conscience.

When we realize that, in the adult male, impotence is the equivalent of castration, we begin to understand the terrors that beset men who enter into sexual relations with beautiful women. Like Faust, they have gambled for immortality, the forever undiminished potency which it is in the power of the original mother-goddess to bestow. But, by seeking her favors, they have violated the taboo surrounding her successor and, at any moment, the dire punishment for that crime may descend upon them. The anxiety so generated inevitably leads to disturbances in function. These, in turn, create new anxieties and further, more severe disturbances. The man caught in such a vicious cycle ends up by psychologically castrating himself.

The fact that his fears are unconscious is what makes them operative in the first place; exposed to the scrutiny of his adult intelligence, they would vanish. Incest, while morally unacceptable, does not cause impotence and, in any case, he has not committed incest. His guilt has as little relation to fact as the phantasies in which it is nourished. But the punishment he inflicts upon himself is real enough and it may drive him to the point of despair. More commonly, however, he rationalizes the situation by blaming his wife or mistress for his predicament. In somewhat different terms, he echoes the cry of Faust: "Her lips suck forth my soul."

As I said before, the beautiful woman cannot be held responsible for these aberrations. She is merely their victim. But they are by no means the only source of her troubles. As a rule, she has already been profoundly "spoiled" by the time she is old enough for an adult relationship.

To understand why, we must consider the vicissitudes of her formative years, the special twist which beauty gives to her development. The process may begin in infancy, assuming—what is frequently the case—that she was one of those extraordinarily pretty babies who stimulate to an absurd degree the narcissistic pride so common among parents. Automatically, this places her in a more favorable position than other children. A show piece from the start, she does not have to exert herself to win attention.

While still very young, she learns the uses of passivity, of being expectant rather than combative. Where other little girls have to battle for their rights, she is precociously aware that an appealing glance and a smile are all the weapons she needs. She becomes a kind of little princess, exacting favors and services from everybody with a minimum of effort. Even small boys, those demons of selfish energy, are impressed by a being so different from themselves. They behave like miniature knights in her presence, conceding her privileges which they would never think of granting to her less comely and more belligerent sisters.

The adult males in her family circle are equally susceptible. Stimulated by that precocious femininity, they respond to her charms as they would to those of a much older girl, sometimes to the point of making involuntary advances. She is much too young to understand what is motivating them and her childish psyche cannot cope effectively with the sexual impulses their immoderate and too frequent caresses arouse. But the fact that such impulses *are* aroused plunges her prematurely into the oedipal situation, with far-reaching effects on her future development. These conquests, at once too early and too facile, may condition her whole method of adaptation. They multiply her chances of remaining fixed at the oedipal level or of regressing back to it when things get tough.

Altogether, this critical period is more highly charged for her than it is for other little girls, and far more dangerous. She may become her mother's rival in fact as well as in phantasy, competing quite overtly and with notable results for her father's favor. On the other hand, he may become so frightened by the incestuous wishes stirred in him by his beautiful little daughter that he brusquely repels all her childish advances.

A rejection so drastic and final is rarely overcome. It accounts for the large number of lovely women who act as though their beauty were a handicap rather than an asset, who cannot be convinced that they have anything to offer to men. They minimize their good looks as far as possible and flinch from attention. Many of them remain spinsters, shy and lonely creatures who lavish on pets the affection which masculinity, in the shape of their fathers, has once and for all time rebuffed.

But the situation is just as bad if the father becomes too enchanted with his daughter, showing his preference for her and, in the process, subtly denigrating his wife. Such a distortion of normal relationships damages the whole family. In the first place, it is apt to make the wife resentful and she may take out her resentment on her relatively helpless daughter. Moreover, the little girl is rarely whole-hearted in her desire to win the oedipal struggle; like a fledgling bird, she is merely trying her wings and she needs to be assured that the nest is intact, an ever-present refuge. However much she may be attracted to her father, it is her mother whom she associates with the idea of home and of love. Her mother's devotion is essential to her security, it makes her feel cherished and wanted and safe, and her father's affection will not compensate her for its loss.

It is possible, indeed, that if the conflict with the mother becomes too acute and distressing, and the little girl's sense of guilt too overpowering, she may retreat from the struggle altogether, accepting sexual repression as the lesser evil. This denial of femininity, coupled with the increasing dependence on the mother, may well pave the way for future homosexual attachments.

Now it is unquestionable that any girl may, in the course of her development, encounter these hazards as well as others. But the threats to healthy femininity are both more frequent and more intense in the case of the unusually beautiful girl. It is not exaggerating to say that the odds are stacked against her to such a degree that her chance of reaching psychic maturity is diminished.

There is one curious anomaly to which the beautiful girl is particularly subject because it is directly related to the over-valuation of the body image. When she discovers, as she does sooner or later, the anatomical difference between the sexes, she is much less inclined than other little girls to feel that she has been defrauded. Her own wonderfully attractive person may make the boy's penis seem, in comparison, a rather insignificant gift. She may even regard it with a certain contempt which, later, is likely to embrace its possessor as well. In other words, she does not envy the man and needs nothing he can give her; her whole person has become a powerful substitute for the missing phallus and, in her adoration of it, she has no room for other emotions.

Her self-love may reach the point where the very thought of sexual relations becomes abhorrent to her, at once a profanation of the beloved image and a kind of infidelity. For a singularly vivid expression of this attitude, let us turn once more to a poet, Stephen Vincent Benét. One of the characters in his long narrative poem about the Civil War is a delicious little Southern belle, Lucy Weatherby. She has scores of suitors but none of them is more enthralled by her beauty than she is herself. Here is Benét's description of her as, about to dress for a party, she stands naked before the mirror:

> "Oh, you honey," she thought, "You honey!
> You look so pretty—and nobody knows but me.
> Nobody knows."
>   She kissed her little white shoulders,
> With fierce and pitying love for their shining whiteness,
> So soft, so smooth, so untarnished, so honey-sweet.
> Her eyes were veiled. She swayed in front of the mirror.
> "Honey, I love you," she whispered, "I love you, honey.
> Nobody loves you like I do, do they, sugar?
> Nobody knows but Lucy how sweet you are.

You mustn't get married, honey. You mustn't leave me.
We'll be pretty and sweet to all of them, won't we, honey?
We'll always have beaus to dance with and tunes to dance
     to,
But you mustn't leave me, honey. I couldn't bear it.
You mustn't ever leave me for any man." *

Lucy, of course, represents an extreme case. The majority of beautiful women, even when they emotionally invest their body image in this way, think of it as a tool rather than an end in itself. It gives them an illusory sense of power, the feeling that, through it, they can exact the fulfillment they crave. The danger is that, in unconsciously equating the body image with the penis, they automatically devalue any man who approaches them, challenging him to match, if he can, what they have to offer. The taunt, though unspoken, subtly conveys itself to him and reinforces his own unconscious equation of the beautiful woman with the phallic mother. Some men are frightened off immediately; the brave ones who rise to the challenge are invariably defeated by the mobilization of their fears. They may revenge themselves for the humiliation they have suffered by degrading the woman, a compensatory mechanism which damages both her and themselves.

Let us assume, however, that the beautiful girl has managed to avoid the most serious pitfalls to which she is exposed in childhood and that she reaches adoles-

* From *John Brown's Body*, copyright, 1927, 1928 by Stephen Vincent Benét, published by Rinehart & Company, Inc.

cence without any marked deformation of character. She is still handicapped on a number of counts, all of them connected with the fact that she has been unduly favored by her environment for a purely passive attribute—her beauty. She has not been required to develop inner resources nor to assert herself as a personality nor to learn what other people are like. The world, as she knows it, is the unreal and effortless world of the dreamer. It is no wonder that dependent, submissive and narcissistic traits—which our society fosters in all girls to a certain degree—become exaggerated in her to the point of caricature. Hyper-feminine, she is only partly a person, and therefore, in a profound sense, not feminine at all.

Badly equipped as she is for life, she enters the arena of adolescent sexual competition confidently, and with exorbitant hopes. In the beginning, they may seem justified. Boys flock around her at parties and she is besieged for dates; her radiant appearance puts all the other girls in the shade. It is a repetition, on a larger scale, of her childish triumphs and it may, if she is lucky, last for some years. That is because, in our society, with its confused and shifting values, girls in their teens are usually given a period of grace. By a kind of tacit understanding—which most adolescent boys respect— they are permitted a good deal of freedom as long as they remain technically chaste. This convention, precarious though it is, helps to postpone a problem which is far more acute for the beautiful girl than for her less attractive sisters. It enables her to fend off, without causing undue resentment, the advances which her looks and her accentuated coquetry invite.

Nevertheless, unless she marries during this period, she has to come to grips with it eventually. Her relations with the opposite sex are never casual, never easy. Other girls have friendships with boys which may, or may not, ripen into romance. They have time to get acquainted, to explore each other's feelings and attitudes, to decide what they mean to one another. The young beauty is "rushed" from the beginning. Boys want to make love to her at sight and very soon do. They compete for her favors. Every date ends with a petting session, every frustrated affair with a quarrel. She is continuously over-stimulated.

No young girl can cope successfully with such a situation. Almost inevitably, she is driven to one of two sexual extremes. If her inhibitions crack under the strain, she has probably taken the first step toward promiscuity; barriers which break down at such an early age are not easily put up again. More commonly, however, her exalted conception of herself, as well as her sensitivity to public opinion, make her want to conform to the socially prescribed pattern, to remain a "good girl." So she rebuffs the boys vigorously, putting a brake on her own feelings in the process and perhaps, in her anxiety, repressing them altogether. She is still waging a defensive war on two fronts but one of them is now unconscious. That furious battle in the depths of her personality lays waste her energies. Later, when she wants to, she cannot "recall" her sexual impulses. She has become frigid.

There are other factors which progressively limit the beautiful girl's capacity to form a stable and satisfying emotional relationship. They are both external and internal and they interact with devastating effect. As time goes on, they even narrow her choices; the sexual partners available to her grow fewer and less desirable.

For all her popularity, she has lost out very early on a sizable segment of the male population. There are, for instance, the nice but inhibited boys. They may dream dreams about her but they keep their distance. The competition is too intense, the light that shines on her too bright. Ambitious intelligent boys also tend to shy off. They know she is expensive and disturbing and, with long years of training ahead of them, they cannot afford to get involved. At most, they have a brief fling with her, raw material for the glamorous memories of middle age. They usually marry somebody else.

The boys who do seek her out are apt to be more sexually aggressive than the average or richer or more neurotic. In any case, they are not disposed to accept frustration and, when they find that they get nowhere with her, they leave her flat. There is, accordingly, a terrific and deeply disillusioning turnover in her relationships. She becomes harder to please, cynical and embittered. Aware of herself as a prestige item, something to show off, she may end up by believing that nobody cares about anything but her looks, that she is incapable of inspiring a genuine affection. In this frame of mind, she may withdraw entirely from sexual competition, ignore her appearance and turn to intellectual pursuits. Or, alternatively, she may try to exploit her charms in some exhibitionistic career like modeling or acting.

Usually, however, her disillusionment is concentrated on her suitors; to herself she still seems the most desirable of women. Meanwhile, as she grows older, her opportunities for making a good marriage dwindle. While she waits for the high and romantic destiny to which she feels entitled, her less attractive friends are becoming engaged to her discarded suitors or to those boys who never circled around her at all. And, though she still has large numbers of admirers, they fall increasingly into rather special types.

Particularly difficult to handle are the "wolves." They want to conquer her mainly because other men have the same idea and they are anxious to demonstrate their superior prowess. Very often, her first complete sexual relationship is with this type of man who is generally skilled in breaking down a woman's defenses. Once he has done so, he quickly loses interest. Engaged in a frantic race with his own unconscious doubts, he has to prove them false by making one conquest after another.

Other specimens of the inadequate male are also attracted to her. There is the profoundly inhibited type for whom, pre-eminently, the glamorous woman is identified with the mother image. He hopes to win from her the stimulus, the "permission" for sexual activity originally denied him in childhood. But, being herself so harried, so confused, she is less qualified than other women to play the role of mother substitute. In fact, she could do with a father herself. If they enter into sexual relations, they are both thoroughly disappointed.

It sometimes happens that, after a number of futile little affairs, the no longer very young woman winds up as the wife or mistress of what may seem to her the "father" type—the elderly successful man of affairs. He is nothing of the sort, of course, but in his own way as unhealthy as the others who are attracted to her. A morbid anxiety has motivated his drive for economic power and still lurks behind the self-sufficient mask he presents to the world and to himself. He cannot let it down. He treats the woman he marries or keeps as simply another acquisition, a valuable piece of property reflecting his acumen and taste. There is no real contact, no love, between them. Menelaus belonged to this type. So did King Mark, and many other deceived husbands. The frigid beauty may be faithful to such a man. Warmer women look for satisfaction elsewhere.

They rarely find it. Neither they nor the lovers available to them are quite up to scratch sexually and desire cannot compensate for lack of capacity. It can only underline the lack. The sorriest aspect of the whole business is that, with each failure to achieve a satisfying relationship, the woman becomes more hostile to the male sex in general, and by her contemptuousness, further diminishes her ability to make a tolerable adjustment. Like the patient whom I described earlier, her very attitude is a threat of castration to every man she meets.

There are men—sadistic or basically indifferent to women—who are not intimidated by this attitude. Their cold contempt, an expression of their alienation, is more than a match for hers and sometimes, if she has come to the end of her psychical rope, she turns to it as a last resort. The people who know her are then treated to an astonishing spectacle, an old fairy-tale come true: beauty enslaved by the beast. Her arrogance wilts; a dreadful and degrading humility takes its place. The man may seem, from any normal point of view, an utterly incongruous choice—a gangster, an obvious psychopath, even occasionally one of those homosexuals who have learned to compensate for their unconscious drives by an excessive display of masculinity. He may inflict the most vicious cruelties upon his submissive partner, steal her money, be flagrantly unfaithful, mock her in public. None of these indignities really matter to her. As long as he maintains his potency, which they serve to support, her attachment to him is unshaken.

In an association of this kind—a horrifying parody of love—the beautiful woman reaches what is for her the point of no return, the ultimate in degradation. But, more meaningful than such a possible disaster, is the

fact that it is rooted in her character. It is the end result of the exaggerated passivity and dependence which
have marked her from earliest childhood and even, by
an ironic reversal, of her grandiose expectations.

The problem of the beautiful woman, when reduced
to its essentials, is the problem of hyperfemininity. As
such, it is not peculiar to her; she merely sets it in bold
relief. Some of the conditioning factors I have outlined
apply to all women. All may apply to any particular
woman, and not necessarily a beautiful one. Just as
some lovely girls miraculously escape most of the obstacles to effective development, so may a quite ordinary
girl encounter every one of them and be correspondingly crippled. It is a question, not of absolutes, but of
probabilities.

The problem should, nevertheless, be isolated because it has an important bearing on the general relations between men and women in our society. As I
pointed out in the first chapter of this book, disturbing
tensions have been created by the sexual liberation of
women and by the elevation, into a social ideal, of the
inherently "desirable" woman. With the help of various
techniques—including, besides the artful use of cos-
metics and clothing, such radical alterations as result
from orthodontia and plastic surgery—more and more
women are falling into this category. As they do, they
acquire many of the characteristics of the authentic
beauty—her heightened narcissism, her extravagant expectations, and her challenging attitude toward men.

Not surprisingly, they also run into many of her difficulties.

There is no doubt that men's reaction to the sexual charm of women is profoundly ambivalent. They desire and dread it simultaneously and, on the whole, they seem to dread it more than they desire it. Most stable cultures—the ancient Chinese, the Mohammedan and, until recently, the Western—have forced women to play down their potential allure. While specific classes were exempted from this edict, notably courtesans and aristocrats, they were surrounded by rigid conventions which limited their contacts with men. Moreover, it was the man who chose the occasion for the contacts, suiting them to his own convenience. He liked thinking about those gorgeous creatures in his spare time, and if he was gifted enough, he celebrated them in art. But, for a lifetime partner, he preferred someone less stimulating. Someone he didn't have to be afraid of.

It is interesting that even today, when beauty is so emphasized, most plain women have no trouble getting married. In this connection, I recall another patient of mine who came to me with a minor disability. About fifty, she was an undeniably homely woman. A comparison of her experience with that of the beautiful patient I described earlier is instructive.

When I asked her about her sex life, she said it had never been a problem. She was then in her second marriage, having been widowed at the age of twenty-seven after four years of happiness with her first husband. She had married again at forty, and the current marriage was equally successful. In the interval between them, she had had a number of affairs, all of them satisfactory from the sexual standpoint. Almost every man who had relations with her told her she was the best sex partner he had ever had.

She had been unattractive even as a young girl, and, to compensate for her lack of charm, had thrown herself into scholastic and intellectual activities, eventually becoming a school teacher. Neither she nor anybody else expected her to marry. She was early resigned to a sexless existence.

However, since none of her many girl friends feared her competition, they regularly included her in their parties. She moved in a literary set where her conversational talents were appreciated. Men liked to talk with her and she never expected them to show any other interest. Yet her friendships with them began to multiply. After she had known a man several months, he sometimes did make sexual advances. Her response, when this happened, was almost one of gratitude.

As a rule, she attracted rather shy men. She did not challenge them in any way and so they felt comfortable with her and quite secure. In fact, several married men with whom she had affairs said they had been impotent for years before becoming involved with her. One of them wanted to divorce his wife in order to establish a permanent relation with this woman.

She told me that the men did not bother too much about her reactions. Most of them, indeed, began by acting as though they were doing her a favor by taking her to bed with them. But both participants invariably enjoyed the experience and usually reached orgasm.

While this woman represents just as extreme a case as my other patient, there are important lessons to be learned from her story. Homely women are safe; they make no demands and they do not arouse threatening phantasies. Men have always been terrified by the sexually aggressive woman and, as far as they are concerned, any woman who stimulates them too much is automatically regarded as aggressive. The great beauty, as we have seen, may be more inhibited than other women are, shyer, less able to cope, but this easily observed fact is lost on most members of the male sex. They judge her by the number of men she attracts rather than by her sexual performance. And especially by the degree to which she attracts them. Just wanting her so much is enough to "suck forth" their souls. If they don't succeed in exciting her, it is a reflection on their masculinity and, if they do, they are afraid that her appetites will be insatiable. In either case, she has placed them in a test situation. Before long, their confidence in themselves crumbles and familiar patterns of behavior come into play—doubts, suspicions, recriminations and, finally, ignominious retreat. The beautiful woman is blamed for the debacle. She is this, she is that, frigid, a nymphomaniac, irresponsible, calculating. The truth is that she makes them uncomfortable and they hate her for it.

H. D., a woman poet, understood the effect of beauty

very well. Like so many others, she was interested in the
legendary Helen and her reflections on the subject are
marked by an insight both sharp and sad:

> All Greece hates
> the still eyes in the white face,
> the lustre as of olives
> where she stands,
> and the white hands . . .
>
> Greece sees unmoved
> God's daughter, born of love,
> the beauty of cool feet
> and slenderest knees;
> could love indeed the maid
> only if she were laid,
> white ash amid funereal cypresses.*

Helen, all the legends agree, was a happy child. Her
mother considered her a divine gift which indeed she
was, since her father was the mightiest god on Olympus.
Though he was not present very much, his beneficent
influence was felt in the household; it enfolded the
small Helen like a sheltering cloud. Her twin brothers
adored her and did everything to please her. Nobody
ever spoke a harsh word to her. She spent her early
years in a delightful daze, anticipating the moment
when a wonderful person, like her father, would arrive
to claim her hand.

* H. D., "Heliodora and Other Poems." Boston, Houghton Mifflin
Company. By permission of the author.

Instead, she was kidnapped by the swash-buckling Theseus who hid her away somewhere until it suited his convenience to get around to her. He never did; her brothers rescued her in time. But, at that, he was probably preferable to Menelaus who was both quarrelsome and dull. And to Paris who never really cared for her. Not to mention the deluded Faustus.

It was a shabby fate for such a glorious little girl. No doubt her mother wept and it is certain that her father and all the aunts and uncles on Olympus were deeply troubled. They tried to interfere but what, after all, could they do? Helen had to live among mortal men who squabbled about her but resented and feared the divinity which seemed implicit in her beauty. Everything that went wrong was her fault, they thought, and in a very limited sense they were right.

Helen, who dreamed too much herself, begot impossible dreams in men. Unwittingly, therefore, she falsified the terms of existence. That is the truth behind her legend and the meaning it holds for us today. But it is not really necessary to be so unrealistic about beauty. Brought down from the Olympian heights on which unconscious phantasy has placed her, the lovely woman is no different from other women, no more divinely gifted, no less feminine. When she is treated as other women are, she will regard herself as other women do and find a real, entirely human, fulfillment.

CHAPTER 5

More Stately Mansions:

The Paradox of Decorating a Home

If you were to ask thoughtful people, including analysts, what they regarded as the crucial situations in a woman's life—the nodal points for a possible breakdown—they would undoubtedly cite marriage, childbirth, menopause and the loss of a beloved person. And they would be right. These are the classic stress-producing experiences, the occasions which—to paraphrase Paine—try women's souls. Each, in its own way, rocks the total personality. If its foundations are defective, as in psychotic individuals, or if the structure built up from them is insecure, as in neurotics, a dramatic collapse may take place.

But there is a special kind of experience which—though it would probably not occur to anybody to mention it—ranks at the top of the list in its capacity to precipitate emotional disorders. Observations I have made in recent years lead me to believe that there is no time at which a woman is more apt to go to pieces than when she is engaged in decorating her home.

The statement may sound ludicrous. It is certainly paradoxical. To set up and decorate her home is every healthy woman's dream, the culmination sometimes of years of effort, the proof of an achievement specifically feminine. That it is so may give us the clue to our paradox. The fact remains that even women who have successfully weathered all the major crises become unbalanced by this experience. In its impact upon an essentially unstable personality, it can be as shattering as an earthquake. The breakdown is occasionally severe enough to require hospitalization of the woman concerned.

I have had the opportunity of observing several such women clinically. That is what first drew my attention to the problem. Once aware of it, I soon found corroborating evidence, not only from other patients but from women who considered themselves thoroughly normal and who rationalized their disturbances in a variety of ways. My own impression—that decorating her home is among the crucial situations in a woman's life—was confirmed and documented in a number of discussions with analytical colleagues. One of them, whose wife was currently going through the ordeal, remarked facetiously that he took his shock machine home every evening—"just in case."

Continued observation has convinced me that the problem deserves serious psychodynamic study. This ordinary and apparently trivial experience seems to present women with a truly great challenge. It puts the woman under tremendous psychic pressure and, in doing so, exposes her underlying weaknesses. Unresolved conflicts may rise up to plague her; basic deformations of character are revealed. Narcissistic attitudes, defects in identification, oral and anal regressions, latent homosexuality, a deeply-rooted sadomasochistic pattern—any or all of these neurotic phenomena may come bubbling to the surface. What form the clinical breakdown will take is, of course, largely determined by the premorbid personality of the patient and by the nature of the defenses she has erected against anxiety.

Before discussing in detail the psychic devils unloosed in the home decorating process, let us admit that less recondite pressures are also operative. Physically, it is an exhausting sort of job and sheer fatigue may temporarily upset the balance of the best integrated woman. Social rivalry, the prestige aspect, is another element in the situation, and unquestionably the source of much nagging worry and doubt. But we can dismiss these universal and easily understood factors from analytic consideration. They are not specific enough to account for the great variety of symptoms and are, in any case, a recurrent problem in the life of most married women.

Nor need we complicate our discussion by including in it other psychic strains which may simultaneously be afflicting the woman who is setting up her home. While it is quite possible that she may be entering marriage at this time, or having a baby, or going through the menopause, these trying circumstances are not essential to the clinical picture. Even when none of them is involved, the home decorating experience may precipitate an active neurosis.

As I said before, it is in itself a profound challenge or, rather, a series of challenges. They are so widespread in their scope and so diverse in nature that there is hardly a woman who can escape facing at least one of them and thus becoming a prey to anxiety. Let us take them up separately, not forgetting, however, that they may appear in combination with even more devastating effect.

As the car is a symbol of masculinity, so is the house a symbol of femininity. To a woman, her home is like another, larger body and all her mysterious impulses find expression within its walls. Her deepest self is implicated in the texture of its draperies, the casual shape of chairs and tables, the dimensions of a bed. As she trudges from shop to shop—examining, comparing, pondering over this article or that—her choices are determined by an unconscious image of what she is, or dreads to be. It reflects the degree to which she does or does not accept herself as a woman.

Most women enter marriage with some residual uncertainties about their sexual role. Unresolved problems relating to their femininity blur the internal image and color their overt behavior. They may be excessively shy or brazenly exhibitionistic; shocked by the strength of their sexual impulses or convinced they are frigid; over-dependent on men or resentful and envious. They may feel threatened by the male genitals, terrified of pregnancy or troubled by a sense of guilt which is the vestigial trace of earlier masturbatory struggles. Though these unresolved conflicts manifest themselves in various ways, they are not severe enough, in the average woman, to incapacitate her or excite more than casual attention. But when she embarks on the home decorating venture, the anxieties attaching to them become suddenly and grossly augmented. Under their onslaught, defenses which have hitherto served her well enough begin to crumble. The problems of interior decoration become hopelessly entangled with her own internal problems, at once borrowing and aggravating the tensions these create.

The home, as I said, is a symbol of femininity. More important, perhaps, from the psychodynamic standpoint, it is a symbol of completely *exposed* femininity. Any wrong notes in its appointments are glaringly evident. They cannot be hidden away in a closet, like an unbecoming dress, or corrected—as a poor job of hair coloring may be—by a hasty visit to the beauty parlor. The expense of home decoration and the time it requires would, in any case, make major alterations impracticable.

The unconscious fear of "exposing" not their taste alone but their inmost selves is what drives a large number of women into the arms of professional decorators. By leaving decisions to the experts, they disengage themselves from the entire project. Or try to, anyway. The attempt is never wholly successful. Some responsibility they have to take, however much they may long to escape it. At the very least, they have to decide what expert to consult. And if the end result is deplorable, they must accept the blame.

This sense of being helplessly trapped, naked to the view of any onlooker, can undermine the woman's defenses. Once involved in the situation, she may stall, put things off, but she cannot get out of it. Except, perhaps, by breaking down. And then, when she recovers, the problem is still there. *Her* problem. Some time or other, she has to make up her mind, choose between alternatives, reveal what she has always tried to conceal, from her own eyes as well as others, her secret self.

Modern or traditional? Rounded lines or straight? Daring colors or subdued ones? Space that is filled or elegantly empty? These are all aesthetic choices. In other words, they express feeling, very largely the wom-

an's feeling about herself. That is why they may become
so agonizing, so disruptive. Or, on the other hand, so
curiously satisfying. Women who decorate their homes
reenter an old unconscious war whose outcome is still
in doubt; every decision they make is a separate engage-
ment, charged with a host of possible anxieties. In the
end, it expresses, directly or indirectly, some buried impulse, attitude or fear.

For instance . . . A girl with a strong unconscious
masculine identification may adopt a starkly modern-
istic décor; its clean straight lines and lack of protuber-
ances announce plainly the kind of body she would like
to have had. But, if she is struggling against this tendency, she may feel a compulsion to "say it isn't so" and
fill her home, as an acquaintance of mine did, with
plump chairs and sofas in the Biedermaier style. This
woman, incidentally, solved her conflict rather neatly.
Her own study—where she pursued her scholarly researches and to which she rarely admitted anybody else
—was, in marked contrast to the rest of her house,
severely functional, with not a curve in sight. It did
not resemble her body which was as stout and cushiony
as the publicly-displayed furniture. But it did give visi-
ble form to the unconscious idea she had of herself, an
idea further manifested in her lean and sinewy prose.

Anxieties about the configuration of the body are
easily, and without any awareness on the woman's part,
displaced upon her furnishings. Breasts, of course, or
the lack of them, are frequently a matter of concern,

particularly so in recent years. The emphasis on large bosoms and the need so many women feel to supplement their natural endowment are carried over into the decorating process. Breast imagery is indicated in a certain bloated kind of upholstery and in the addiction to piles of fluffy cushions. But it may also be represented in reverse, obviously in rooms where every piece of furniture is severe and unyielding and, more subtly, by a predilection for faint and epicene curves.

Any part of the body may be singled out in this way. A middle-aged matron, whose legs were markedly bowed, changed her living-room three times before she could come to terms with her obsession about them. The first time, the tables and chairs had legs as bowed as her own. They were beautiful costly pieces and everybody admired them but they made her obscurely uncomfortable. She got rid of the lot and substituted others with delicate straight lines. These bothered her even more. Finally, after months of wracking indecision, she disposed of her problem by buying the kind of modern furniture which is all massive blocks and has no legs at all!

Another woman, preoccupied with her bowel movements, treated her whole house as though it were a gigantic bathroom. All the walls were bare and white and the curtains were made of some transparent plastic material. Decorative bowls, also white, and rather oddly shaped, rested on every available flat surface. A crowning touch, in which she took great pride, was a small foun-

tain set up in the wall which had originally held a fire-
place.

A specific problem of this kind is often concentrated
on a specific decorative feature—as, for example, the
clock, which may be treated as a symbol of the female
genitals. Its hidden inner machinery is easily equated
with those recessed and thus mysterious organs and its
rhythmical movement is reminiscent of their periodic
activity. There are women so obsessed by their genitalia
that they put clocks all over the house or, conversely,
hesitate to display even one. These different ways of
handling the same obsession depend on the varying patterns of exhibitionism in the women concerned.

Unconscious exhibitionistic tendencies may determine the entire character of the home. A woman may
have a strong impulse to display herself and yet be
ashamed of her personal appearance. If her self-love is
great enough and her financial circumstances permit it,
she will make her house the showpiece she herself is not.
The frustrated impulse finds an outlet in interiors
which are exquisitely ostentatious, a delight to the eye
of the beholder. Everything is carefully chosen, beauti-
fully kept and in its appointed position. Not a hair, we
might say, is out of place. It is obvious that a home of
this kind is not well adapted to daily living. The woman
who has designed it will not tolerate disorder and is
constantly nagging at her husband and children. They
are made to feel like interlopers—as, indeed, they are,
in a sense. There is no room for them in her phantasy.

Her house is not really a home; it is the lovely woman she has always longed to be.

Extreme narcissism, however, may defeat its own purposes. For women who are inordinately vain, the problem of decorating their homes is sometimes quite insoluble. The case of one of my patients illustrates the dilemma in which they are caught. Her appearance absorbed her to such an extent that she had had her nose altered by plastic surgery, not once but a number of times, all of them unnecessary. She spent literally hours a day in front of the mirror, studying her face and figure from every angle. When she began to decorate, she showed the same excessive concern, brooding over each detail, changing her mind constantly, paralyzed by doubts. The magnitude of the task in itself overwhelmed her, since her self-absorption left her little time to spare for it. In addition, she was thoroughly baffled by her unconscious need to create, through the home, an idealized image of herself. In a desperate attempt to master the problem, she enrolled in a school for professional decorators. But her goal still eluded her and, after a while, she broke down completely, developing paranoid symptoms severe enough to send her to the hospital. This happened several times. As soon as she started to make some headway, panic overcame her and she had to be hospitalized again. She never succeeded in finishing her home.

Exhibitionistic attitudes may also be revealed in the treatment of exteriors. Some women—especially those

who have unresolved conflicts relating to their fertility
—put their major efforts into landscaping and garden-
ing. Others show their unconscious drives by an over-
emphasis on large picture windows. These make archi-
tectural sense when they enclose a breath-taking view;
when, on the other hand, they front on the street, they
encourage any casual stroller to look inside. By contrast, there are women who turn their homes into
veritable dungeons or choose to live in remote and inaccessible places where they are safe from observation.

If the home-making process starts from scratch—if
the house is built to order or carefully selected—another important aspect of femininity comes into play.
That is the woman's capacity for emotional contact, the
degree of closeness to others which she is able to sustain.
A home may be arranged to foster intimate relationships, as when the kitchen is large and inviting enough
to become a center for family activity and the sleeping
quarters of its separate members are clustered together.
It is also quite possible, even in a relatively small house,
to fix things in such a way as to insure a large measure
of privacy.

There are schizoid homes where closed doors are the
rule and each member of the family is effectively isolated from the others. At the opposite extreme, there
are homes in which nobody can count on an hour's
solitude. The woman who has solved the problem of
"closeness" in genuine accord with her psychological
needs is in a fortunate position. The reverse is fre-

quently true. A warm outgoing woman may be compelled by circumstances to live far from neighbors or in a cold secret house. And a woman who is unable to endure continuous emotional interplay may find herself in a family and a community from whose pressures she cannot withdraw. Either of them may crack up under the strain. As a matter of fact, a considerable number of our patients today seek therapy for disturbances which originate in this problem.

The decoration of a home requires a good deal of money. Newlyweds often put all they have into the project; other families may devote to it a considerable portion of their savings. That alone weighs heavily on the woman who is actually doing the spending. Quite apart from the fact that attitudes about money are closely linked to a number of neurotic conflicts, she knows that she cannot afford to make any major mistakes. If she does, they will be staring her in the face for many years to come.

A responsibility of this kind is particularly hard on obsessive personalities who tend, in any case, to demand too much of themselves. Reacting, in a compensatory fashion, to unconscious feelings of guilt, they are unusually scrupulous, careful and orderly. Their finicky conscience is always ready to upbraid them; unless they are convinced that whatever they are doing is "right," they feel miserable. But the determination of just what *is* right leads them into endless speculations and soul-

searchings. They cannot make snap judgments or act
upon the basis of emotional impulse. Every decision has
to pass through a tortuous mental loop, be examined
from all sides, weighed against any possible eventuality.

For such women, the innumerable choices forced
upon them by the decorating process cause unmitigated
torment. Some of them bog down at the very beginning,
putting off—from week to week and month to month—
the necessary preliminary steps. Others start over and
over, drastically altering their original plans as new and
what they cannot help thinking are better ideas occur
to their harassed minds. Meanwhile, as time goes by
and their tensions increase, they find themselves less
and less able to cope with the situation. Often their
homes remain uncompleted. These are the women
who, in the ordinary course of affairs, are constantly re-
arranging their furniture, so obsessed sometimes that
they get up in the middle of the night to try out some
new grouping. But they are never satisfied. The next
day, or the next week, they are at it again.

In severe cases, the obligation to act, to do *something*,
becomes locked in a hopeless conflict with the need to
be right. Unable simply to drop the job, and equally
unable to decide what to do about it, the woman sinks
into a deep depression. This serves a double function;
it simultaneously takes her out of the battle and punishes her for her cowardice.

What defeats these women, who might otherwise have
overcome their indecisiveness, is the money problem. If,

owing to unresolved conflicts, their attitude about money is emotionally charged, they are very likely to become panicky when they have a lot of it to spend. In the first place, the average woman is not accustomed to massive expenditures. As she goes about her shopping, and the money pours out of her hands in what seems to her frighteningly large sums, she may become overwhelmed by the responsibility. It is her life-blood, and that of her husband and children, which is draining away.

The lack of standardization in the decorating field is another source of confusion. A woman's ordinary expenditures, for food and clothing, are predicated on fairly stable values. She knows a good buy when she sees it and she is quick to snap up a bargain. But, in buying for the home, she is confronted with a wide range of prices for substantially the same item. It is not only the difference between wholesale and retail and the varying percentages of decorators' discounts; it is that all these price levels are in constant flux. Nothing seems to have an intrinsic worth. With no norms available to guide her judgment, she becomes disorganized, sometimes losing all sense of proportion. She spends too freely or too frugally and she cannot get over the idea—occasionally quite justified—that everybody is out to cheat her. With every purchase, her anxieties mount.

Home decoration presents still another hazard to the obsessive type of woman. The disorder that attends it,

like a mangy and persistent cur, is in itself enough to
drive her out of her wits. The need to have things clean
and under control is as much a part of her character
pattern as the tendency to indecision; she will worry
about dirt and disarray in the same way that she worries
about money matters. The chaos she is caught in at this
time strains her compensatory mechanism to its limits.
She soon finds that all her careful prearranged sched-
ules are useless; nothing works out in the way she has
planned. Certain necessary articles are impossible to
locate, others fail to arrive at the promised time. Care-
less and dilatory workmen add to the confusion. Meanwhile, her daily routine is disrupted, her children run
wild and her husband gets the sulks. Everything that
made up her private world seems to be falling into ruin.

The desire to create, to make something that was not
there before, lies deep in women; it is a component of
their biological nature. But it becomes linked to something more personal, the need to express *themselves*.
It is true that the majority of women, like the majority of men, are not artistically gifted. The impulse
has to find some less emphatic outlet—in the way they
dress and do their hair and make up their faces, in
cooking and needlework and other shy round-about
terms. And most of all, for women, in the arrangement
and decoration of that larger self, their home.

Women who are uncertain and anxious about their
taste may try to run away from the challenge, taking

refuge in a bland admission of incompetence. They delegate the job to others—mother, husband, or professionals—or resolve their dilemma by making their homes as indistinguishable as possible from the homes of others in their circle. While this use of accepted formulas may relieve their anxieties, it does not dispose of them altogether. Almost always, it leaves a residue of shame. Put to the test, they were found wanting.

Yet their problem is not nearly so acute as that of the woman who takes pride in her artistry and who has been anticipating for years the opportunity to show what she can do when given a free hand. That woman is really on the spot. Particularly if she has been in the habit of voicing critical comments on other women's taste. Or if friends and relatives have regularly turned to her for advice. Everybody now expects a great deal from her. Not least, she herself.

As a consultant, such a woman may have demonstrated both artistic capacity and practical know-how. But, when the problem is her own, and with the whole world, as it were, looking over her shoulder, it is quite possible that her assurance will wilt. If she is at all obsessive, she may be paralyzed by indecision. Or become so disorganized that she cannot get anything done. Or begin to have doubts about her creative powers. All the "blocks" that afflict talented people, the psychic barriers that get in the way of expression, may rise up to impede her progress. One of my patients, an excellent and fairly successful artist, went into a "benign" hysterical stupor every time she tackled the job of decorating her home. It took her five years, two of them under analytic treatment, to complete it.

That state of suspended animation is not uncommon. But there are other ways in which creative women may respond to this particular challenge. Some, in their anxiety to prove themselves, to avoid the ordinary, go so far in the opposite direction that their homes have the grotesque quality of a surrealistic painting. I remember one nightmarish living-room, like an underwater cavern in its gloomy beauty. The walls were a strange deep blue-green, with tanks of tropical fish recessed into them. The tanks were brilliantly lit and the fish darted about in them like living jewels. The only other light came from some hidden source in the ceiling; it drifted down as from another world. Bleached driftwood and hunks of ghostly coral lay about everywhere. Instead of chairs, there were divans, so low and wide that one could not sit up on them. It was a room not to live in but to drown in.

Unfortunately, the women who perpetrate these interesting horrors *have* to live in them. So do their families. The painter can wipe off his canvas, the writer rework a chapter or toss it into the waste-paper basket, but the creative housewife is compelled to contemplate her errors indefinitely. That is the main reason why decorating is such an ordeal for her. She is afraid to let herself be carried away by the ideas that leap into her mind. The moment's fine frenzy is one thing; to have it take permanent shape is another.

Up to this point, we have focussed almost wholly on the effects home decoration has on the woman's relationship to herself. That is where, psychodynamically, the emphasis belongs. But it may be worth while to consider briefly certain situations where the relationship between her and other people places an added stress on her capacity to handle the experience.

The concepts of home and mother are closely linked, so closely that, in the unconscious, they are sometimes indistinguishable. Here lies a special challenge, almost a threat, to the young woman who has just been married and is, simultaneously, establishing a home. The act implies maturity. It is a final declaration of independence from her mother, a tacit announcement that she herself has now achieved equivalent status and is ready to be mother and home-maker in her turn. The trouble is that, psychically, she may not be ready at all. The anxiety she feels about her new role is then transferred to the setting in which it will be enacted. And, for obvious reasons, it will be manifested most clearly in her relationship with the woman who remains for her the symbol of home, her mother.

Traditionally, in our society, the wife's family assists the young couple in the decoration of their home. While the assistance may be largely financial, the mother usually has an active hand in the job, dispensing advice, joining in shopping forays and otherwise making herself useful. Inevitably, there will be some differences of opinion, minor clashes of no great significance in themselves. But, if the daughter's attitude toward

her mother contains some morbid residues, they will
flare up like tinder to the spark in the emotionally
charged atmosphere. Old resentments will burn anew
—feelings of having been neglected or dominated, or
edged out in the oedipal struggle. They will give a
passionate undertone to a discussion about draperies,
embitter an argument over the size of a bed. Without
quite knowing what is happening, mother and daughter
are reenacting a long forgotten battle.

Unacknowledged feelings of dependency may also be
reactivated. Anxiety makes many young women—who
think they have liberated themselves from their mother's influence—become helpless children again, unable
to take a step without her supporting presence. Or,
reacting against a need of which they feel ashamed, they
may reject her help altogether. Paradoxically, then,
they will turn to some other older woman and unconsciously transform her into the maternal figure they
have consciously rejected. The unresolved struggle for
liberation will continue on a new and still more meaningless plane.

More damaging than this situation, however, is its
opposite—where the daughter, through the circumstances of her marriage, suddenly becomes the dominant figure in the relationship. If she is richer and
happier than her mother ever was, if she needs nothing
that her mother can give, she has, in a sense, displaced
her and the original outcome of the oedipal struggle
is reversed. Her home, so much lovelier than the one

she has abandoned, provides a painfully concrete proof of her victory. No matter how much pride the mother may take in her daughter's achievements, no matter how gracious the latter's hospitality may be, the shift in their relative positions cannot fail to produce tension in both. In the daughter, the reawakened feelings of guilt are sometimes abnormally strong, so strong that she has to punish herself. One young woman I know symbolically "undid" her triumph over a period of years. Every time her beautiful home approached completion, she destroyed what she had already accomplished and started the process anew. The external confusion reflected her emotional disorder and, at the same time, preserved her mother's superior status as a home-maker. Other women alleviate the anxiety aroused in them by this situation by persuading their husbands to move to another community.

Just as decorating her own home often causes a resurgence in the woman of unresolved problems connected with her mother, so may it bring to a head underlying tensions between husband and wife. Because the strain on the wife is so great, it is frequently a time of great marital turmoil. That, in turn, accentuates difficulties hitherto unacknowledged or minimized. Usually it is money that sparks off the conflict. The husband may become increasingly disturbed as he watches his wife floundering in the financial bog, at one moment foolishly worried about the cost of some

particular article, at another spending with what seems
to him hysterical abandon. If, in an attempt to reassure
her, he allots more money to the project than he had
planned to originally, his generosity is misinterpreted
as a reckless disregard for the family's future. If, on the
other hand, he puts his foot down, he is accused of being stingy and authoritarian. An attitude of amused
tolerance will not help him either; besides alienating
his wife, it will probably provoke charges of gross selfishness and indifference.

All these reactions on the part of the wife testify to
the deep-seated anxiety mobilized in her by the decorating process. But, as the bewildered husband sees it,
she is simply trying to put him in the wrong. So, nine
times out of ten, he loses his temper and, in the tempestuous arguments that follow, the relations between
them are stretched to the breaking-point. What may
have been conceived as a mutual experience, an expression of their profound "togetherness," only serves to
drive them apart.

The situation confronts the husband with a dilemma
which, in spite of his best efforts, he cannot resolve. One
of my patients made that clear in describing what happened to him. He was frank to admit that he was a
man of limited taste, unqualified to make aesthetic
judgments. He was quite content to leave the decorating job to his wife in whose capacity he had implicit
faith. His part in the venture, as he saw it, was to foot
the bills. But this separation of function was unaccepta-

ble to the wife. After a short indoctrination course, she convinced him that he, too, could recognize and enjoy aesthetic values. They were then ready to proceed on a mutual basis. Since the wife had more leisure, she did the preliminary leg-work and only called in her husband for the final decision. As time went on, he became more confident. Assured by his wife that his opinion really mattered, he began to disapprove of some of her choices. To his astonishment and dismay, she became violently enraged, taunted him with his lack of taste and went on from there to devalue him in other ways as well. She had built up his authority for only one purpose—to bolster her own judgments and thus mitigate her anxiety. As soon as he disagreed, it spurted up like a geyser. In her scalding attack on him, she projected doubts about herself which had nothing to do with the matter at hand.

The average husband, during the decorating period, regards his wife as a crazy woman. For her part, she considers him an unfeeling lout. There is more than a grain of truth in both assumptions. But, when contempt is so openly expressed, it leaves deep wounds. They are slow to heal.

I remarked earlier that many women try to disengage themselves from the tensions of home decorating by putting the whole difficult business in the hands of professionals. This is a clear case of jumping from the frying-pan into the fire. Unless they have unlimited financial resources and can remove themselves from the picture altogether by going on a long trip, they are in for a singularly traumatic experience. Any feelings of insecurity—and such women are basically insecure—will be seized upon by the experts. They have learned how to play upon the personality of their clients and they will twang away ruthlessly at its defective strings.

The professional decorating field, along with its allied trades, has become a happy stamping-ground for misfits of all kinds, among them a large number of homosexual males and vigorously aggressive females. These people are fundamentally hostile to the normal purposes of home-making; children, family life in general, are outside their range of interest. Moreover, they are working in a viciously competitive field and, whether they are genuinely gifted or merely in it for the money, it leaves its mark on them. Their behavior is notoriously high-handed. It simplifies their operation when they can undermine any confidence the client may have in her own judgment and they have developed skilled techniques for reducing the refractory ones to a pulp of submissiveness. The least sign of opposition to their sometimes bizarre ideas, the smallest protest about costs, sets off a counter-barrage of formidable power. The offending client is treated to temperamental flare-ups and studied insults and, unless she capitulates instantly, further punished by a variety of delaying tactics.

Nor can the woman count on her husband for support. In the majority of cases, he refuses to be drawn into a situation which he considers beyond his scope and competence and which, unless he is irritated by the attendant confusion, he is apt to regard with a good deal of amusement. His lack of interest and bantering comments are a further trial to his poor wife but there is no doubt that, from his own point of view, he does well to keep aloof. In the rare instances where husbands let themselves be persuaded to enter the fray, they are almost invariably outmatched by the professional consultants who know the weak points of the ordinary male and are artful in deflating him.

The woman who tries to solve her own decorating problems is spared the lethal barbs of the experts but she is spared little else. The allied trades, as I said before, are also swarming with misfits. Among the assorted workmen she is obliged to deal with—the plasterers, painters, paper-hangers and plumbers—there is a disproportionately large number of paranoid personalities, men who seem to bear a permanent grudge against the human race. They do not trouble to disguise their hostility; it manifests itself in sullenness, rude and intemperate language and, frequently, in sloppy performance as well. When reproved, they are as likely as not to walk off the job, leaving everything in an unholy mess and softening up their bewildered customer for her next persecutor.

The average woman is dismayed and baffled by this paranoid challenge, which she can neither avoid nor cope with. She is equally disturbed by the more subtle attack of the homosexuals whom she encounters in shopping for various decorating specialties. As a rule, she has previously had very limited contact with this type of man and is only dimly aware of the hostility behind his ingratiating manners. Nor does it dawn on her that its target is the entire female sex. Talked into buying things she has no use for, harassed by inexplicable delays and by the delivery of wrong or defective goods, a miasma of suspicion begins to cloud her mind. She feels personally abused, chivvied and cheated on every side. To these feelings is added a sense of helplessness, the conviction that she is simply not up to the job. No wonder if, in such circumstances, her defenses totter.

In the realm of commercial relationships, there is probably none which compares, in sheer malignancy, with that which exists between the woman who is decorating her home and the people who supply the advice and materials she requires. For a woman who may have latent paranoiac tendencies, this damaging relationship can be quite enough to tip the scales. Her intimates do not always recognize the gravity of the situation and aggravate it with ill-timed jokes. Since the initial suspiciousness has a realistic base—as it is true of most paranoid reactions—its pathological components may not become fully apparent until the breakdown is well advanced.

The disturbances associated with the decorating experience are not trivial. They deserve to be treated as seriously as any other emotional upheaval. I have found that, by doing so, many patients are able to recognize their unconscious problems and come to grips with them.

CHAPTER 6

Taboo:

The Paradox of Masturbation

Analysts have long known that there is one act which even their most sophisticated patients are reluctant to talk about. These people may discuss other sources of shame with comparative freedom. They will, for instance, admit that they hate their parents . . . that they are unfaithful to their mates . . . that they regard their children as an intolerable burden. They will concede sexual inadequacy, give expression to homosexual fears, own up to a variety of perverse and sometimes dangerous impulses. But, however candid they may be otherwise, they rarely confess to masturbation. Not in the present tense, anyway. Both men and women shy off from the subject, using every device of circumlocution in the process. Months of therapeutic contact are usually necessary before they can be induced to face up to it as a current problem.

It is paradoxical that so widespread a phenomenon should arouse such exaggerated feelings of guilt and shame in the average patient. It is likewise paradoxical that, with so many aspects of the problem still unclarified, there is comparatively little discussion of it in the scientific literature. We do not know much more about masturbation today than we did in 1912 when Freud—leading a seminar on the subject—called it "inexhaustible." The scarcity of new contributions to this important field of research points to the existence of an inhibiting factor. That factor, undoubtedly, is the drastic taboo on masturbation which, in one way or another, has always prevailed in Western culture.

Before we go on to consider the historical permutations of that taboo, it might be well to make one point clear. There is nothing inherently "unnatural" about the sexual stimulation of the self. Most children indulge in the practice and so do many animals. It is tolerated in some cultures, encouraged in others. Informed observers today generally agree that masturbation in childhood, far from being harmful, represents a normal phase of development and is, in a sense, a preparation for the mature sexual act. They also agree that its pathological significance in adult life is symptomatic rather than causative. Masturbation, in other words, does not lead to neurosis; it may be one indication, among many, that neurosis exists. The adult who makes a habit of masturbating, like the adult who habitually eats to excess under emotional tension, has remained fixed in or reverted back to a childish pattern of behavior.

There is a difference, however. The pattern to which the glutton regresses, though more infantile, has always been regarded as natural at a certain period in life—nobody, after all, objects to a suckling baby!—and thus carries less guilt. Masturbation, while equally natural, was vehemently discouraged from the very beginning of the Judaeo-Christian culture. The taboo, which originally had the character of a religious proscription, declares in effect that children are not—or should not be—sexual beings. The recognition that they are, and that the genitals are capable of pleasurable sensations long before they are ready for the reproductive function, is a fairly recent finding in our culture. It is to the genius of Freud that we owe the rediscovery and description of childhood sexuality.

Why did our primitive forefathers suppress it so thoroughly? The answer to that question lies buried under the debris of thousands of years. While many theories have been advanced, they are all in the realm of speculation if not, indeed, of myth. But current anthropological research and the behavior of civilized peo-

ple in conditions of stress indicate that, when an individual, a family or a society is struggling for survival,
sexual freedom is a luxury which is foregone almost
automatically. The uninhibited pursuit of pleasure—
in children as well as adults—not only takes up a lot
of time in itself but drains away energies which can
be channeled into more utilitarian directions.

Most primitive peoples have survival problems and
it seems probable that the interests of the community
as a whole dictated some limitation of sexual activity.
Over-population in subsistence areas is a factor; so is
the need for economic manpower and for defense
against invasion by neighboring tribes. Group ambition
may also be a motive. There is little doubt that sexual
suppression in childhood fosters the development of
strong and closely-knit family units and these, as I have
pointed out in a previous chapter, are a characteristic
of the most effective and enduring cultures.

The cohesive family prevailed among the ancient
Hebrews whose moral values, while somewhat attenuated, are still an integral element in Western civilization. Sexual taboos were early incorporated into their
religious structure; even adult intercourse was encouraged only if it fulfilled a procreative purpose. The
sin of Onan, as described in the Old Testament, was
that he spilled his seed on the ground. (Onanism has
become a synonym for masturbation as well as for the
ejaculation with withdrawal which was its first meaning.) It is not hard to understand why an agricultural

society, like that of the Hebrews, should compare semen to seed and deplore its waste; the human crop was as valuable to them as anything they grew in the fields. Numerous children, in their opinion, were proof that the family stood high in the Lord's favor. This belief, it may not be too cynical to remark, is intimately linked to the fact that children, as unpaid helpers in the fields and with the flocks, contributed materially to the family's prosperity.

Children who are permitted free sexual development are not apt to be docile instruments. They tend to mature early and set up establishments of their own just when they become real economic assets. Their parents cannot dominate them beyond the period of biological need, having failed to set up the necessary psychic ascendency. When, on the other hand, sexual impulses are inhibited at an early age, the parents' authority is felt for a much longer time, possibly for life. Rather than risk the loss of their love and protection, the young child will conform and, in time, their prohibitions become internalized, replaced by the sense of guilt which is the foundation of what we call conscience. The individual then renounces sexual play not only because he is commanded to do so but because he feels in his heart that it is wrong.

This dependency constellation is the basis of the patriarchal family structure which, in turn, is elaborated in the religious doctrines of monotheism. A stern deity takes over from the parents, perpetuating the pattern for succeeding generations. Whatever its original motive, it was their program of sexual inhibition which distinguished the early Hebrews—and, later, the Christians—from their pagan neighbors. The mechanism of self-denial and atonement for lapses played a crucial role in the development of their ethical system, with its stress upon mutual responsibility, the obligation which every member of the human family owes to his fellows. It also built up that tolerance to frustration which is such an important aspect of the civilizing process. The individual who has learned to defer the fulfillment of his sexual drives may be in a better position to withstand other frustrations as well.

The idea that masturbation was "sinful," a moral offense, prevailed for many centuries and, among those people who accept it, is still a powerful deterrent. But, around the time of the Reformation in Europe, the religious argument seems to have lost some of its authority and a new method was introduced to maintain the taboo. Since it was based on the fear of physical injury, we might call it the hypochondriacal sanction. Masturbation gradually came to be regarded as an act not so much against God as against the self. It was "hurtful," leading to weakness and, perhaps, to even graver disturbances.

Discussion of its presumed ill effects began to fill the medical literature and, by the nineteenth century, practically every disease of unknown origin was attributed to excessive indulgence in this "dangerous" habit. Masturbation took the blame for epilepsy, insanity and cancer; it was believed to doom men to premature impotence, women to sterility. Doctors, as well as laymen, considered it the outstanding cause of every type of physical infirmity.

As medical knowledge increased, however, this sanction, too, diminished in force. The spread of the germ theory—with its proof that specific micro-organisms were responsible for specific diseases—removed much of the terror associated with masturbation. So, even more, did various scientific developments which occurred around the turn of the twentieth century. Freud's researches into childhood sexuality, anthropological studies of other cultures which permitted masturbation, the knowledge that it is practiced by a number of animal species—all these findings helped to dispel the belief that the act of self-stimulation is, in itself, injurious to the body.

The hypochondriacal method of repression took its last-ditch stand in the theory—to which Freud himself clung for many years—that masturbation leads to so-called neurasthenia, a vague syndrome supposed to result from some damage to the sexual apparatus. That theory has, in its turn, been abandoned but it is a striking fact that the prohibition persists, giving ground in one field only to reappear in another. The anxiety about masturbation appears to be so deep-seated in our culture that some excuse can always be found to justify the mechanism of denial.

The current emphasis is largely psychological and, while it may not be so effective in maintaining the taboo, it induces feelings of shame and unworthiness by subtly capitalizing on our existing sexual mores. According to modern doctrine, there is nothing "wrong" about masturbation; certainly it does not cause either physical or mental injury and it would be foolish to brand such a harmless impulse as immoral. But—and this is the new line—it's kid stuff. Quite normal in childhood and early adolescence, of course, deserving tolerance if not encouragement as a transitional and educative phase in the sexual awareness of the self. Not normal in adults, however. Under ordinary circumstances, if full heterosexual maturity has been reached, there is no longer any need or any desire to masturbate. The individual who does feel that need and that desire automatically convicts himself of sexual inadequacy. He is "infantile," a failure in the most important task of life.

Now all this is deeply humiliating, more humiliating to the sophisticate, perhaps, than to less enlightened individuals. Other infantile modes of behavior are mercifully veiled in symbolism but the adult who masturbates or wants to masturbate cannot disguise, even from himself, the naked childishness of his act. What was once a sin—the bold defiance of a punitive authority—has been devalued to the point where it is simply but acutely embarrassing, and he hesitates to admit it as he would hesitate to admit that he wet his pants. Under the consciously-felt embarrassment, however, the old unconscious guilt still lurks, evidence of a taboo which is no less operative because its sanction has again been altered.

The fact that masturbation is, for one reason or another, a "forbidden" practice may result, paradoxically, in its being used for purposes far removed from the primary one of achieving sexual pleasure. A person who is intellectually sophisticated and has, at the same time, a strong masochistic drive may engage in the act for the very reason that it humiliates him. There are patients who masturbate whenever they have to acknowledge failure in some crucial life experience, thus expressing and completing their sense of degradation. Secondary psychological motives of this kind are not, as we shall see later, uncommon. To understand the phenomenon of masturbation, we must consider such hidden motives for the act as well as its significance in sexual development.

For the young uninhibited child—as for the primitive and the animal—masturbation is fun. He plays with his sexual organs because he gets pleasure out of doing so and for no other reason. But, like so many other playful activities, self-stimulation serves an important developmental function. It is a technique of mastery, a method by which the child discovers his body and its capacities—for sensation, for excitement, for rhythmic movements and for coordinated skilled activity in general. He learns how to recognize inner tensions and how to handle them independently. Enjoying his own body, he comes to value its potentialities as he will come, later, to value the potentialities of other bodies.

There is a question in the minds of many investigators whether, strictly speaking, this early period of genital play should be called "masturbation." It is frequently non-orgastic and, according to Rene Spitz, flourishes only when there is an optimal relationship between the child and his mother during the first year of life.

It is in adolescence that masturbation becomes—for the boy, in any case—of major educational importance, preparing him, both physically and psychically, for his future sexual role. Gradually, setting his own pace, not blocked by the need to impress anybody, he conditions his body to the intense pleasure of orgasm. And, as he does so, phantasies spring up in his mind—vivid, confused delightful images of how it will be some day, how it *is*, with a girl. With time, and as his physical confidence increases, the phantasies grow more exact, closer to the reality which, as yet, they only approximate. Through masturbation, he tests his maturity and brings it into being. There is no possibility of avoiding this fundamental experience altogether. If consciously suppressed, it will be carried out in the dream life—with

far greater distortion in the accompanying imagery—
and result in the incompletely realized orgasm of nocturnal emission.

This solitary dreamy phase of sexual preparation is
normally succeeded, in our society, by one which—
while still on a fairly masturbatory level—involves a
partner of the opposite sex. In the experience of petting
and necking, phantasy almost touches reality. The most
important aspect of the experience, for the developing
boy and girl, is that it allows them to feel the sensation
of orgasm in each other's presence, not alone any more
but together. The usual problems of adolescence—
shame, unfamiliarity with the opposite sex, fear of being humiliated by it and disgust at coming into contact
with its genital organs—all these can be worked out
in the process of courtship. Once they are resolved, both
boy and girl are readier than they would otherwise be
to enjoy the mature sexual act.

But are these preliminary experiences essential? For
the male sex, I think, it can be said that they are. I
doubt that any man can reach full sexual maturity without them. The man who has never consciously produced an orgasm, either by stimulating himself or in
petting, is almost bound to be impotent when he attempts intercourse. Some transitional experience—beyond that of nocturnal involuntary orgasm—seems to
be absolutely necessary for his development. Most men,
of course, go through the whole cycle I have described.
Personally, I know of only one case in which the pre-

liminaries were by-passed with any degree of success.
This man, who grew up in a slum section, started to
have intercourse on a regular basis at the age of thir-
teen.

In general, however, such premature assumption of
the adult role is extremely damaging. The great majority of young adolescents are simply not ready for the
experience, however big and tough they may seem.
They may be pushed into it by environmental pressure
but, with rare exceptions like the man I have noted,
they cannot perform adequately. Instead, they are
swept into a pattern of repeated failures which often
endures for life and which they try to cover up by
adopting aggressively male attitudes. A terrific anxiety
prevents them from masturbating and they are too
arrogant to seek help from the women against whom
they continuously and vainly pit themselves. Some of
the most severely impotent men I have encountered in
practice conformed to this type. Having missed the
slow ripening which adolescent masturbation encour-
ages, they had become not the men they wanted to be
but only gross caricatures of manhood.

For women, the problem is quite different. There
seems to be very little correlation between their sexual
development in early life and their capacity to enjoy
a mature heterosexual relation. Many women, in fact,
who have masturbated actively in childhood and derived orgastic satisfaction from petting and necking
turn out later to be relatively frigid in intercourse.

Others, paradoxically, with little or no preparation of this kind, make an easy adjustment to their adult role and find great fulfillment in it. I am not suggesting that a negative correlation necessarily exists between early and mature sexual activity in women. What I mean to say is that we cannot predict, as we more or less can for men, the course their development will take.

The reason is that women are more complex creatures physiologically. They have not one sexual organ but at least two and the one they discover and take pleasure in first is of lesser significance. Most little girls are not even aware that they possess a vagina; their interest centers on the clitoris, a vestigial organ which serves no reproductive purpose but which can be stimulated, like the penis, by masturbation. Once this point has been noted, however, the parallel breaks down. While the boy's preliminary orgastic experiences are applicable in adult life, the girl's are not. Clitoral orgasm does not educate her for vaginal orgasm. It seems, indeed, that to achieve the latter she must go through an obscure *re*-educative process which involves modifying the gratification she has previously known. That shift in psychic interest is by no means automatic; many women fail to make it and others do so only late in life.

Another complicating factor is that the woman is far more diffusely sensual than the man. The satisfaction which, for him, is concentrated from infancy to senility in the penis filters throughout her body. Mouth, breasts, buttocks, bladder, the entire area of her skin, are excitable to a degree which makes them, for orgastic purposes, supplementary sexual organs. Yet, with all this overwhelming potential, she may never be sexually awakened. For she is, to a large extent, dependent on her partner—not only on his capacity as a lover but on the emotional climate in which the love-making takes place. Where his pre-genital experiences are determining, hers are, at most, of contributory interest. Like Galatea, she needs a Pygmalion before she can come to life.

I have been discussing masturbation in its normal aspect, as a prelude to mature sexuality. But, as I remarked earlier, its "forbiddenness" has had certain paradoxical consequences. In both children and adults, masturbation may become a neurotic device, the indirect expression for needs and impulses which may not be specifically sexual in character. The pleasure premium is then subordinated and sometimes it is even forfeited altogether. Let us see how such a curious eventuality may occur.

When we commit a forbidden act, we automatically defy those who have forbidden it. In the case of masturbation, it is the parents first of all whose authority is flouted, against whom the child rebels. For the sake of a pleasurable sensation, he risks disapproval and even punishment from the people upon whom he depends. Wordlessly, he is declaring his *independence,* announcing, in effect, that the satisfaction he gets from stimulating himself is more important to him than remaining in their good graces. That self-assertion and defiance may, in the end, become the chief motive of the act.

In early childhood, certainly, masturbation is as much an expression of the ego as it is of sexual impulses. I have noted its significance in the child's discovery and mastery of his body. By the degree to which it helps him to establish a separate identity, to find pleasure in himself rather than exclusively from others, it marks a symbolic withdrawal from the parents, the beginning of self-sufficiency. If they intervene to stop him, he must either obey them—and, perhaps, dam up forever his impulse to explore, to act independently— or rebel.

Adolescent masturbation usually carries the process a step further and is often a factor in the progressive estrangement between the child and his parents. The breakdown in communication, so characteristic of this stage of development, makes it difficult for the adolescent to confide in anybody, least of all in the parents who were originally responsible for the prohibition. He masturbates with all the guilt that he felt in childhood and, if his anger against the parents is deep, with increasing defiance. Symbolically, he is telling them just where to get off and, in his excited self-justification, he may no longer derive any positive pleasure from the act.

This masturbatory pattern, in which guilt and hostility combine to drive out the feeling of pleasure, may persist into adult life. There are marriages in which one or the other partner, or both, resort to masturbation whenever serious tensions arise between them. In doing so, they point up their alienation from each other and prolong it. It is as though they were saying, with childish spite: "I don't need you. I can play with myself." Most people who masturbate in this frame of mind have phantasies in which the sexual act is permeated with violence and hatred, becoming an aggressive assault against the imaged partner rather than an expression of warmth.

When masturbation is habitually used to express anger or defiance, it stops being altogether enjoyable. But there is an even more harmful consequence. The individual who has made this crippling association loses the capacity to assert himself in a normal way. Instead of acting to change the disturbing situation, he masturbates, withdrawing more and more into his phantasy life, a progressive detachment which gradually unfits him for healthy relationships and even, in extreme cases, for participation in a competitive society. Masturbation, in such an individual, unconsciously perpetuates an ancient battle, long terminated in fact, the battle against his parents. By doing so, it succeeds in fusing and thereby blunting the two most powerful drives in his, as in all human nature—sex and hostility.

Some anxiety about the genitals is universal in our culture and, perhaps, in every other culture as well. The anxiety begins in childhood when little girls wonder, with varying degrees of envy and resentment, why they have not been endowed with a penis and little boys are afraid that they will lose or hurt theirs. These fears are exacerbated if threats of injury are incorporated in the technique of discouraging genital play. While the threat has more significance for boys than for girls, the latter, surprisingly enough, are not immune to its terrors. Some of them even think that the punishment has already taken place, a phantasy which may lurk permanently in the unconscious, with deleterious effects on their development.

What is most interesting, however, is that few children of either sex give up the forbidden practice completely. The more scared they are, the more will they be tempted to masturbate, if only to reassure themselves that their genitals are still intact and functioning. In time, a vicious repetitive cycle is established in which masturbation leads to fear and fear to renewed masturbation. It is not fun any more but a compulsive ritual whose only purpose is to exorcise the terror to which it has itself given rise.

While the preoccupation with genital injury subsides as the child grows older, the hypochondriacal pattern remains, etched deep in the mind. One of its more obvious manifestations is the syphilophobia of adolescence, a curious and for the most part objectively meaningless dread. The adolescent who suffers from it shrinks from sexual contact and often from any physical contact at all but things are happening in his body which he cannot control and these things, he feels unconsciously, are punishable. As a rule, this dread also subsides in due course though many adults are so frightened by the possibility of venereal infection that they surround intercourse with elaborate precautions or avoid it altogether.

In most cases, however, the sexual content is repressed and substitute organs become the focus of anxiety. The fully-ripened hypochondriac has completely forgotten his original fears; the panicky protectiveness he once felt for his penis is now lavished on his stomach, his heart or his kidneys. He may still masturbate on occasion, compulsively, without pleasure, too worried, perhaps, to realize what he is doing. It is a fluttering heartbeat that engages his attention or the dull pain in his guts. Yet he is reassuring himself in the same old way and he is making the same psychic sacrifice of enjoyment. In the persistence of that childhood pattern, his real motivations are revealed.

The physical pleasure of masturbation is sometimes not so much lost as inundated, swept out of consciousness by a wave of uncontrollable emotion. Orgasm is a tremendous experience and, in its first impact on the child, may be so overwhelming that it induces panic rather than satisfaction. That is particularly true if his earlier masturbatory activity has been limited so that he discovers the sensory capacities of his body in the confused and turbulent context of adolescence. It is as though, having known only the placid waters of a lake, he were suddenly tossed into the ocean. Or as though—to bring the image closer to the actual experience—the little kitten he has been stroking should assume, without warning, the terrifying beauty of the king of beasts.

An occasional child will be shocked enough to give up masturbating altogether, thereby postponing—sometimes permanently—the effort to come to terms with his body. In others, the struggle with masturbation is linked to the general adolescent struggle for emotional control. If they cannot give up the practice, they become disorganized and fearful, profoundly convinced that they are "losing their minds." Their school-work suffers as they seek refuge from their over-strained feelings either in obsessive rituals or in a clinging dependency on their parents. The young person who is unable to cope with the emotional aspects of masturbation is well on his way to an anxiety-ridden future. As he grows older, his attempts to tame the "animal" within him may result in the construction of such elaborate defenses that all his energies become neurotically bound, incapacitating him not only for sex but for daily life.

On the other hand, too much control is as bad as too little. The adolescent whose sexual impulses give him no trouble whatever, who slides through puberty with ease and aplomb, merely testifies to the strength and rigidity of his inhibitions. Later in life, he will find it difficult, if not impossible, to tap these deeply buried feelings and, perhaps, other feelings as well. He will be unresponsive, "unfeeling," cold. When emotional resources are so heavily guarded, they become—not only inaccessible, like the gold at Fort Knox—but useless. It is not too much to say that, in the attitude toward masturbation, the whole economy of the personality is involved.

Let us look at the experience from another angle, its potentially isolating effect. As I noted earlier, the impulse to masturbate may be the signal that the child is beginning to break away from his parents. That emotional detachment is not lessened by the fact that incestuous phantasies of a crude and sketchy kind often accompany the act of self-stimulation. The guilts they arouse are themselves alienating and thus serve to accentuate its clandestine and lonely nature.

With the resurgence of the impulse in adolescence, the child may feel so culpable and so afraid of exposure that he gradually withdraws from all significant human ties, those with his contemporaries as well as those with his family. The tendency to do so will be stronger if he is unaware, as many young people are, that the habit is not confined to him. It is not unusual for the adolescent to believe that he, and he alone, commits what he may consider—if he is at all religiously inclined—"the unpardonable sin."

The process of withdrawal sometimes gains momentum through the myth, commonly accepted, that masturbation is readily detected. The worried young person may have heard that it causes, to cite a few examples, stooping shoulders, rings around the eyes and even, absurdly, the growth of hair on the palms of the hands. Such disturbing rumors are not critically appraised; the guilty mind is a credulous mind, so obsessed by the need to hide its thoughts that it can neither observe nor analyze clearly. The great danger the adolescent faces is that, in his frantic desire to escape detection, he may fall into a self-perpetuating pattern of withdrawal —with masturbation leading to loneliness and loneliness, in turn, prompting further masturbation.

This is not to say, however, that loneliness in itself precipitates the impulse to masturbate. Recent studies indicate that, if the feeling is intense enough, sexual interest of any kind wanes. According to Spitz, the child who is deprived of warm human contacts masturbates less than the average child, an impression confirmed by investigation of the sexual behavior of isolated groups. Frank reports that soldiers stationed in the Aleutians went through periods of profound inhibition and Friedman noted a similar indifference among the inmates of concentration camps. These findings, nevertheless, do not invalidate the point I wish to make—

that, the shame and fear induced by masturbation may cause the adolescent to isolate himself.

Another kind of pattern emerges if he knows that his contemporaries—particularly those of the same sex—also indulge in the forbidden habit. He may then draw closer to them in common defiance of the parental figures. Many children share the experience in secret talks and, occasionally, in mutual stimulation. By acting together, and thus pooling their anxieties, they often succeed in overcoming them. There is always the possibility, however, that attachments made at this level of development will persist into adult life on a homosexual basis. Since the gratification received is at once sexual and social, the drive toward a normal interpersonal relationship loses some of its force. In individuals already predisposed to homosexuality, the experience is probably clinching. It removes any remaining incentive for turning toward the opposite sex and thus the chance which adolescence offers—to correct the earlier faulty identification—is permanently lost.

While masturbation, when mutually engaged in, may result in overt homosexuality, we should not overlook its far less obvious use as a defense against homosexual tendencies. Many men and women who shrink from relations with the opposite sex drain off, by masturbating, the impulse to turn to their own. Others who have conquered the impulse sufficiently to establish a heterosexual relationship but still have some unresolved conflicts about it manage to maintain their equilibrium by occasional secret indulgence in the act. This brief digression points up the indubitable fact that masturbation is, for the most part, as solitary an occupation as dreaming. The adult for whom it is the only or predominant method of obtaining sexual satisfaction is in abject flight from human relationships. Real people are too much for him, too stubborn, too demanding, requiring an expenditure of emotion which, in his neurotic impoverishment, he cannot afford. When they enter his phantasy at all, they are wraiths, deprived of their hard living substance, shattered to bits and remolded "nearer to the heart's desire." The compulsive masturbation associated with certain severe psychotic breakdowns shows the mechanism of flight and autarchy at its extreme point of development. For the schizophrenic, turning away from a world he finds alien, his sexual organ is like Aladdin's lamp; he uses it to summon up a genie—his own distorted imagination—who will fulfill his infantile wishes and thus give him the mastery he craves. And the enormous relief.

The relief of extreme tension, which may or may not be sexual in origin, is sometimes the chief motive for masturbation. Orgasm may be induced, in other words, not so much for its climactic pleasure as for the "dulling" which follows it, the profound relaxation of body and mind. That same "dulling" is probably the reason why mental deficiency and even epilepsy were formerly blamed on excessive masturbation. It also accounts for the fact that people who feel guilty about it often complain of chronic fatigue. The fatigue is a neurotic elaboration by means of which they unconsciously punish themselves for indulging in the practice.

There are people who become "addicted" to masturbation as they might be, in different circumstances, to sleeping pills or alcohol or morphine. This aspect of the problem seemed so striking to Freud that, in one of his letters to Wilhelm Fliess, he called masturbation the "primary addiction" for which all the others are only substitutes. Certainly, there are some marked resemblances—the temporary "lift," with its stimulation of phantasy, the subsequent lethargy and the flattening of normal emotional reactions. In the kind of psychotic patients I mentioned earlier, the capacity for feeling has been channeled almost completely into the masturbatory act. They are not only withdrawn but absorbed and there is no way of engaging their attention or interest. Like zombies, they are emotionally dead to the world.

A long-standing and powerful taboo still surrounds the subject of masturbation. No aspect of sexual life is more complicated and yet so little discussed or understood. While its developmental function is generally recognized, we cannot be sure that it should be allowed to proceed unchecked. For, as I said earlier, its inhibition has had incalculable effects on the character structure of Western man; and there is no doubt that, in any civilization, the capacity to defer gratification is what distinguishes the healthy person from the impulse-ridden psychopath. At the same time, it is plain that the profound guilt reactions sometimes induced by pro-hibition may precipitate grave disturbances not only in sexual function but in other areas of life as well.

One large question has been left dangling in the air. Is masturbation in adult life always a symptom of maladjustment? Does it, in every case, indicate that the individual has either failed to achieve maturity or re-gressed to a lower stage of development? To answer those questions, we need only to ask some others.

Under certain conditions—in wartime, at sea, in prison—large numbers of men are thrown together for protracted intervals and no women are available. Should these men masturbate or turn to each other for sexual satisfaction?

In the happiest marriages, there are times when hus-band and wife are deprived of each other and thus of the sexual outlet each would normally prefer. During separation and illness or—to take the most common in-stance—in the period just before and after the wife's de-livery of a child—marital relations are impossible. Is masturbation to be considered normal in such circum-stances? Or is an extra-marital affair the healthier alter-native?

The childbirth situation, with all its emotional over-tones, poses the problem with peculiar forcefulness for the man, as is illustrated by the experience of one of my patients, a twenty-nine year old writer. An only child, rather undisciplined in his habits, he had entered analysis for a work block. His background was casually Bohemian and, since he was a good-looking young man, he had had quite a lot of affairs during his late adolescence and early manhood. This free-wheeling sexual activity had come to an end with his marriage, in the previous year, to a very attractive and competent girl. Their relationship was a good one and, on the day his problem emerged into focus, his wife had just given birth to a boy.

My patient came to see me directly from the hospital, proud and happy but also concerned about the rough time his wife had gone through. Toward the end of the session, however, his thoughts veered away from her and toward his own sexual abstinence in recent weeks. It would be so easy, he remarked, to call up one of his old girl friends. With his wife in the hospital, there was no need to make complicated arrangements, no danger of discovery. And, after all, he wouldn't really be hurting her. . . . He was arguing himself into infidelity.

The next day, he told me what actually happened. His sexual tension had mounted and, by evening, he could think of nothing else. He picked up the telephone. But, with his finger on the dial, he abruptly changed his mind and decided to masturbate instead, something he had not done since the age of fifteen. It made him feel foolish, he said, and yet it seemed better than being disloyal. There was no question in my mind that, under the circumstances, this apparently regressive act was the more mature choice for this man.

For the adult who cannot permit himself to masturbate, whose anxiety about the act is so great that he would rather indulge in an emotionally meaningless affair or turn to a homosexual relationship or deny himself altogether, is not proving his maturity at all. Instead he is simply proving the major paradox of masturbation —that the infantile fear remains a power over which he has no control.

CHAPTER 7

The Roving Eye:

Paradoxes of Male Infidelity

What makes a man unfaithful? Why, having freely chosen one woman as mate, does he turn for sexual satisfaction to others? I am not speaking of men who, through a variety of circumstances, are separated from their wives for long periods of time. Nor of those whose wives are chronically ill or so neurotic that they shrink from physical union. Nor even of the seriously disturbed individuals in whom infidelity is only a secondary symptom of a deep-lying emotional disorder. The latter have been well documented in the classical case histories of psychoanalysis and the discussion of their problems is a matter for the textbooks. The men I am concerned with here are apparently healthy and acceptable to the women they have married. They have homes, children, attractive wives, jobs, a settled position in their communities. Quite ordinary men, in short, leading what seems on the surface like ordinary lives.

Now there is little question that many men, faced with an unexpected opportunity for sexual adventure, will be tempted to make the most of it. Occasionally, perhaps, they will succumb to the temptation and enjoy it without attaching too much importance to that temporary lapse. But, on the whole, they will feel rather sheepish about it and they will not make a habit of such extramarital adventures. Certainly they will not allow themselves to become really entangled with women other than their wives. That is because monogamy, while by no means a law of nature, is so firmly entrenched in our society that the average man cannot kick over the traces without some sense, however attenuated, of guilt. He may be humorous about his defection or defiant or argumentative but, no matter how skillfully he rationalizes his behavior, some uneasiness persists.

Habitual infidelity thus implies a rebellion against a complex cultural pattern which the individual may or may not endorse intellectually but with which he is, as a member of his society, inextricably identified. The person who cannot tolerate a monogamous relationship may not be severely neurotic. But, as analysts have generally emphasized, it is neurotic components in his character structure which make him unable to curb his random sexual impulses in the interest of more stable and enduring satisfactions.

That those impulses exist is indubitable. Anyone's unconscious, when thoroughly explored, yields evidence of them. But awareness of that fact does not lead to infidelity. When unconscious processes are subjected to analysis, they lose some of their compulsive character. The individual who has gained insight into himself is not as helpless as he was before, not as much at the mercy of irrational drives. He knows that it is foolish to let impulses have their way without regard to his personality as a whole. He also finds it harder to find spuriously noble or reasonable motives for behavior which is essentially undisciplined. No longer so bound, so deluded, he will hesitate to endanger relationships which have proved their value.

Infidelity usually serves part of the personality at the expense of the whole. But the most fundamental paradox of this phenomenon is that interests not predominantly sexual are also implicated and that, in the resulting conflict, the pleasure which is its conscious purpose is often forfeited. It is this aspect of extramarital sexual activity *without "fun"* which is our present concern. The compulsive purposelessness of the behavior and its self-defeating end-results are what interests us.

Why, then, to return to our original question, are

men unfaithful? When we realize that a multiplicity of factors—many if not most of them unconscious—are involved, the problem becomes as complicated as the personalities of the men concerned. Yet we may venture some generalizations. I have already indicated that basic cultural attitudes influence the situation. But specific environmental pressures are even more important; they must be taken into account if we are to understand the "why" and "how" of extramarital episodes. As observed in the New York area, the men who habitually indulge in such episodes break down into four main clinical types, each of which has some distinctive features and special paradoxes of its own. While there is bound to be some criss-crossing in individual cases, the classifications are by no means artificial. By illustrating them in terms of particular men, I hope to present a graphic and easily recognized picture which will clarify the determining features of each.

Traditional Type

When Arthur B. first came to consult me, he had no intention of talking about his sexual problems. As a matter of fact, he did not even recognize their existence. Forty-three years old, he was a handsome forceful man with that elusive quality which is known in the theater as "presence." In his own view, he was very masculine, a belief which afforded him considerable satisfaction.

But there were other, more solid reasons for his self-esteem. The star salesman of a family-owned plumbing firm, he was proud of his success in that highly competitive business. He was also proud of his pretty wife, his two teen-age children and the large apartment in Brooklyn in which he maintained them. Financially indulgent, he was strict in all other respects. The children were well brought up, he said; they attended a religious school and no loose talk or behavior was permitted in the home. That was the way he had been brought up himself and he had never had any cause to regret it.

What induced this apparently stable man to seek psychiatric treatment? Well, there was one thing that worried him, he admitted, his blood pressure. It jumped about erratically, sometimes reaching dangerous heights. He was mortally afraid it might result in a stroke or some kind of coronary attack. His doctor had spoken about tension and cautioned him not to drive himself so much, relax a bit . . .

Though he fought off the knowledge, Arthur's inability to relax had a sexual origin. Unconsciously, he was at war with himself. For years, almost from the beginning of his marriage, he had been leading two distinct and incompatible lives. In one, he was the respectable head of a household, a devoted if somewhat self-righteous husband and father. In the other, he was an incorrigible woman-chaser. Arthur not only believed in the double standard; he practiced it to the hilt. He became enraged if his wife even looked at another man but he was continuously unfaithful to her. Every time he "went out with the boys," as he did at least once a week, he ended up in some amenable woman's bed. The more abandoned they were, the better he liked them. Sexually, that is. They meant nothing to him in any other way. All his affections were centered on his family, and particularly his wife.

She, of course, knew nothing of his escapades. Her own relations with him were tepid and conventional; she had never been sexually awakened. Arthur made few complaints on that score. Though he occasionally cited her coldness as a justification for his infidelities, he would have been disturbed rather than pleased if she had exhibited any ardor. He had married her because she was "pure" and that, in essence, was how he wanted her to remain. Good women, in his opinion, were not interested in sex. They lent themselves to it to please their husbands and in order to have children. Arthur approved of these aims, just at he approved of marriage as an institution. But monogamy was something else. According to him, no real man could take it. It was contrary to nature.

There was no conscious sense of guilt in Arthur. As he saw it, his behavior was thoroughly normal, a conviction bolstered by the fact that all his cronies behaved in the same way. Far from hurting his wife, he felt, he was showing consideration for her in channeling his sexual drive toward loose women. Yet a couple of remarks, casually dropped in the course of treatment, revealed the depth of his inner discomfort. Whenever he returned from one of his extramarital adventures, he bought special little gifts for his wife and children. He also made a point of his excessive cleanliness, observing that he took a shower both before and after intercourse. Without being aware of it, he was following a ritualistic pattern of atonement and purification. As his mounting blood pressure indicated, it was not enough to ease his conscience.

It is obvious that, to men like Arthur, there is something inherently dirty about sex. Dirty and at the same time fascinating. They can come to terms with it only by separating the sensual from the affectionate side of their natures, drawing a ruthless line between the "bad" women who attract them and the "good" women they revere. That ancient and familiar dichotomy—sacred as against profane love—has remained a psychic reality to them. That is why I have called their type of infidelity "traditional." Deriving from the values and inhibitions of a patriarchal society, it strikes an oddly anachronistic note in the contemporary New York scene. These men seem never to have heard of Havelock Ellis; they are unaffected by the revolutionary tides which have swept over the old-fashioned family structure and, in doing so, have altered profoundly the most intimate relations between men and women. Early conditioning of a specific sort has immunized them against the prevailing sexual mores.

It is needless to say that the men who conform to this purely traditional type are neither highly educated nor given to intellectual pursuits. Most of them are engaged in some personal trade or business, frequently, as in Arthur's case, a small family enterprise. Their attitude toward brainy people, "eggheads," is cold and a little contemptuous; they regard professional career women with suspicion and are uncomfortable with those from a higher social level, whose "classiness" they resent. Since they rarely open a book after leaving high school and have no close associations outside their own kind, there is little to challenge the assumptions they have carried over from childhood.

We find such men most often among the sons and grandsons of immigrant groups which have managed to maintain much of their identity by insulating themselves from the larger culture around them. Even after they have become moderately prosperous, they resist assimilation, clustering together in neighborhoods which bear the stamp—sometimes subtle, sometimes blatant, but always unmistakable—of their point of origin. Their children share a common background, attending the same schools and religious institutions, having the same habits, exposed to the same parental admonitions. When they grow up, they marry one another, or boys and girls from similar backgrounds, thus perpetuating the group pattern for another generation. As it applies to the family, that pattern is patriarchal, however much the different groups may vary in other respects.

In an earlier chapter, I described some of the motives and characteristics of the patriarchal system. Most important, in its impact on the developing boy, is the fact that at no time does it occur to him to regard his mother as a sexual object. In so far as she is a desirable woman, she is the exclusive property of a father whom he has been taught to venerate and fear and with whom, as a consequence, he would not dare to compete. Quite commonly, however, in families of this kind, she is not a sexual object even to her husband, being valued and valuing herself only with respect to her maternal role. Thus the boy's incestuous desires—normal at a certain stage of development—are either nipped in the bud or prevented from budding at all. If, in his innocence, he turns to other females in the family environment—sisters, cousins and aunts—he soon finds out that they, like his mother, are strictly out of bounds. Drastic punishment makes it clear to him that, in the home situation, any sign of sexual interest is taboo.

That taboo has momentous consequences for the boy. In later years, it will rise like an invisible barrier of thorns between him and every respectable girl. He will marry one of them in due time but it will not occur to him to seek sexual fulfillment in her arms. Only "fallen" women—those who have placed themselves on the other side of the thorny barrier—can satisfy impulses which have been so decisively deflected from their original objects and their original setting.

Deflected, but by no means suppressed. While female

sexuality is frowned upon in the patriarchal household, male sexuality is merely driven elsewhere, kicked outside as it were. Arthur B. had a lusty and powerful father who encouraged him—by example if not actually by precept—to prove his own mettle. He was barely fourteen when he had his first experience with a woman, visiting a brothel with several other boys and, later, comparing notes with them. The experience was not particularly pleasurable but it made him feel, as he put it, "like a man." He repeated it at intervals, whenever he could save up enough money from his allowance; by the time he was eighteen and earning a salary, it had become a regular Saturday night practice, an established group activity. On one occasion, he contracted gonorrhea. He shrugged his shoulders in telling me about it, as though to dismiss its importance, but his exaggerated cleanliness seems to have had its origin in that misfortune. At about the same time, he stopped consorting with prostitutes, satisfying himself with the accessible women he met in the course of business and an occasional pick-up at a bar or night club. He could spot a loose woman at a glance, he told me, and there were always plenty of them around.

With minor variations, Arthur's boyhood history is the history of other men of his type. As described by Kinsey, they go through a relatively brief struggle with masturbation which ends early in adolescence and does not again arise to plague them. Their entry into heterosexual relations is not always as deliberate as Arthur's—

it may be precipitated by a seduction—but it is, almost invariably, premature. It is also lacking in emotional warmth. The emphasis is on the physical act alone; there is no real relationship between the partners, no tenderness, no esteem, not a trace of romantic exaltation. A furtive business, to be gotten over with as quickly as possible. That abrupt and brutal awakening deepens the cleavage, already present in the boy's mind, between sex and home. Emotionally speaking, he has been cut in half. The dichotomy in his attitude toward women stems from a dichotomy in his inmost self.

It often happens, in these premature contacts, that the boy encounters some difficulties in performance. Mocked by his more experienced companions for his failure to meet their inflated standards, his shame is intense. The need to prove himself, to be male, is paradoxically converted into what is, in essence, a grotesque sibling rivalry, a determination to be as good, or better, than the other fellows. Years after that early failure has been forgotten, it will motivate his amatory behavior. Neither before nor after marriage will he turn down a chance to show his stuff. For such a man, every act of infidelity is a vindication, a triumphant retort to the scorn he once endured from his contemporaries.

However, the traditional type—driven though he is, and fundamentally disappointed—may manage for years to maintain a fairly stable balance. By keeping his two worlds apart psychologically, he is able to derive satisfaction from them both. For emotional security, he depends upon a family structure not very different from the one he knew as a child. Having picked out a suitable woman, he marries her with the not unreasonable expectation that she will run his home adequately, bear his children and not challenge his masculinity in any way. A certain chilliness on her part does not displease him; it gives him a convenient excuse for his gambols and assures him that, like Caesar's wife, she is beyond reproach. His own demands on her are limited, just enough to preserve his franchise as a husband; by the time he reaches middle-age, they will probably have ceased altogether by mutual consent.

In marked contrast to this dreary sexual routine, the man's extramarital activities are orgiastic in their abandon. The women he seeks out are not only sexually provocative but from backgrounds as alien as possible to his own. If they are socially inferior as well, so much the better. His need for them is purely physical, uncomplicated by affection or romantic strivings. The less they remind him of home, the more uninhibited will his impulses be. And, since the last thing he wants is to be "discovered" by his wife, he will be careful to keep his relations with them on a casual, temporary and clandestine basis. To him, they are essentially degraded creatures and he has a horror of becoming involved with them.

Once in a while, that happens. His unconsciously calculated defenses give way and he falls in love, as helplessly as any schoolboy, with one of these "bad" women he is constrained to despise. Whether or not she is in love with him, too, he cannot trust her; he is tortured by doubts about whom she is seeing and what she is doing in the hours and days he must spend away from her. Will she find somebody she likes better, some man more potent and more generous than himself? If he can afford it, he may try to resolve his predicament by setting her up as his mistress, buying by this means the exclusive right to her favors. Then, if all goes well—if his mistress convinces him of her fidelity and their relationship is regularized—an extraordinary situation develops. The "love nest" becomes another home for him, his mistress a second wife. In effect, he duplicates the original setting; then he again feels the need to betray, this time the second "wife."

Most men of the traditional type do not fall in love with the women they use sexually. But it is in uncommon cases of this kind that the underlying paradox of their behavior is most clearly revealed.

His boastful and aggressive masculinity is a disguise, a kind of sexual wolf's clothing under which is hidden a terrified sheep—the small boy he once was. He withholds desire from his wife—the "good" woman—because he unconsciously equates her with the mother who was placed out of his reach in childhood by a more than ordinarily stringent taboo. Through identification with his father—he is now a family man himself, with a home of his own—the taboo is partially lifted but not enough to make him comfortable in the relationship. It is fear that makes him turn to other women and not, as he thinks, unbridled lust.

It is fear, too, though of a different kind, which largely determines his attitude toward these women. Since they lack the inhibitions which he considers normal in females, they seem to him sexually powerful creatures, a threat as well as a stimulus to his manhood. It is only sporadically that he feels able to meet their challenge. In labelling them "bad," he makes use of an ingenious protective device. The emotional response which normally accompanies the sex act is blocked off, leaving him free to suit his own convenience and needs without regard to theirs, without any sense of obligation to them as human beings. By devaluing them, he guards himself against being overwhelmed and his wife against comparison with more desirable women.

Desirable to him, that is. She may actually be a warm and attractive woman whom a less twisted man would find eminently pleasing. It is not my purpose here to consider her reactions and the values of a marriage so precariously maintained. What must be obvious, however, is that the man's behavior is, in the end, self-defeating. Since he is not an integrated personality, he cannot engage himself wholly with any woman and, since he cannot engage himself wholly, his relationships become progressively thinner and more meaningless. As he grows older and his sexual interest wanes, he finds no compensating affection to take its place. Occasionally, however, this type of man in later years manages to salvage some degree of security if he has managed not to offend his children by his behavior toward their mother. He frequently rejoins the family unit and his wife as the doting grandparent who gives his grandchildren the love and interest which he could never fully lavish on his own family.

Narcissistic Type

Charles D. was a charmer. I am not referring to his appearance, though that was attractive enough in a lean well-groomed country club style. It was a trick he had of concentrating the whole weight of his attention on whoever he was speaking to, of seeming to give himself to that person, and that person alone. He used it on me at our initial interview. After studying me for a moment, he said, with a candor that was obviously meant to impress me: "I'm drinking too much, Doctor. It's getting to be a bit of a problem."

I had noticed his shaking hands, the red streaks in his eyes, the blurred look which alcoholism gives to the features. He knew I had noticed them. But to be candid about such damaging facts, when they cannot be concealed, is a trait not uncommon among narcissistic personalities who tend, in any case, to make assets out of their defects. The neuroses from which they suffer originate very early in life and, from the standpoint of

treatment, are both complicated and unrewarding. It is
not my purpose, however, to discuss therapeutic questions. What I would like to demonstrate here is the pattern of infidelity found in men of this type and the kind
of social background in which it flourishes.

In the course of twelve years of married life, Charles
had seduced his wife's older sister, the majority of his
wife's friends and an amazing number of other women,
including the wives of several business associates and
clients. There were also a few actresses. As a top-flight
advertising executive, with TV and radio accounts, he
met plenty of them but, on the whole, he preferred
women from his own social circle. Both in town and in
the surburban community where he lived, there was no
lack of opportunity for a man with his persuasive talents. He had, however, a tendency to be indiscreet
which was further aggravated by his heavy drinking.
Time after time, he missed serious trouble by a hair.

Charles did not want his wife to divorce him, as she
had threatened to do on a number of occasions, moved
less by his infidelity than by his alcoholic rages. Financially, she was independent of him; she came from a
family of enormous wealth and she and their four children were protected by income of her own over which
Charles had no control. It had been rather a feat to
marry her at all since his own family, though socially
pretentious, was in modest circumstances. They would
never even have met except for the exigencies of wartime which placed him in California where she was ac-

customed to spend the winter. A handsome young executive, he did not find it hard to ingratiate himself with a girl who had no particular physical charm.

To do Charles justice, he was as much impressed by her accomplishments as a sportswoman as by her wealth. Their romance actually began on the golf course, in a mixed doubles tournament. She was still an amateur golfer of note and, in recent years, she had also become an ardent club-woman. Though her prominence in the community was a source of great satisfaction to Charles, it led indirectly to their most bitter quarrels. Absorbed in her own concerns, she left the care of her home and children to a staff of increasingly incompetent servants. The household was disorderly in the extreme and, at the same time, so extravagantly run that Charles' more than adequate income barely sufficed to cover its expenses.

If there had ever been any real feeling between Charles and his wife—and on his part, at least, that is doubtful—it had long since evaporated. Now in their late thirties, they continued their untidy life together partly on account of the children, partly out of habit and partly because neither of them could envisage anything much better. To Charles, it seemed a quite tolerable relationship on the whole, threatened only by his excessive drinking. Why he drank so much, why he was consistently unfaithful and why his wife showed no interest in their home were questions he never asked himself. They were simply facts and he accepted them without curiosity, as he accepted the emotional emptiness of their joint existence. From his point of view, he was a pretty lucky man. If he had not quite reached the pinnacle of what to him seemed success, he was at any rate close to the top.

That marked shallowness of affect is characteristic of men of his type. Emotionally incompetent, undeveloped, they do not look for intrinsic satisfactions. What they want is to be "important" in a social sense, sought after, envied, in the swim. Considerations of prestige dictate all their choices, determining where they live, what work they do, the restaurants they patronize and the women they pursue. Money, in itself, is not their goal; they would rather be a junior member in some distinguished law firm than the sole owner of a prosperous canning factory. Sex, for its own sake, is not their goal either. A woman who does not enhance their position, who lacks that indispensable attribute of prestige, leaves them cold, however desirable she may be otherwise. Like Charles—who seduced his wife's sister and her friends and the wives of *his* friends—they tend to confine their adventures to their own social group. That is the most striking aspect of this type of infidelity.

These men have generally been conditioned from childhood to exclude most of the human race from their system of values. The family ideal—whether or not it can be carried out in practice—is to "belong," to be counted among the glamorous and privileged few. The children are brought up in conformity with that ideal, to which everything else is subordinated. They learn very early that what they feel and think is of far less moment to their parents than the impression they make. Since the emphasis is all on display, good manners take precedence over more solid virtues and a good seat on a horse is rated higher than intellectual distinction. The other children they meet are measured in terms of their clothes, the schools they attend and the make of the family car.

As a rule, there is very little emotional warmth in such families and not much contact between parents and children. Charles told me, with a laugh, that his mother had laid the groundwork for his success with women by teaching him, as a very small boy, how to kiss a lady's hand and how to circulate agreeably at a cocktail party. But, as far as he could recall, she never took him on her lap and hugged him and, when he was sick, a maid attended to his wants. If he was frightened or worried about anything, he kept it to himself; it did not even occur to him to go for comfort to his parents. He started attending summer camps when he was eight and boarding-school when he was ten. Though the family was only moderately well off, his education was that of a rich boy. It was important, his father said, to make the right connections.

Making the right connections, being seen with the right people, doing the right thing remain life-long needs for the narcissistic male. Like the pool into which his prototype looked, they serve as a kind of mirror in which the idealized image he has of himself is reassuringly reflected. Without that distorting mirror, his pretentions would collapse; the "prince" would be revealed as what in fact he is, an emotional pauper so blunted by want that he cannot even reach out for the affection he unconsciously craves. Throughout his childhood and adolescence, he is engaged in a continual struggle to control feelings which are at variance with that exalted self-image. He is unwilling to appear at less than his best; hurts and fears are covered up, doubts unacknowledged. A barrage of smart chatter drowns out the whimper of pain.

Sexually, the premarital background of such men varies considerably. There may be some contact with promiscuous women, some homosexual episodes, either overt or unconscious. Prolonged masturbatory activity is common, its privacy effectively hiding the loss of control. The dating pattern revolves around the most popular girls, the ones who can be flaunted triumphantly, shown off like a rose in a buttonhole. Beauty in a girl is an asset at college proms but social eligibility is even more important.

In the choice of sexual partners, narcissistic identifications are often apparent. In contrast to the traditional type, there is a tendency to choose women who are not too female, epicene small-bosomed types with athletic proclivities and an apparent absence of maternal drive. In making love to a woman of this type, the young man is unconsciously making love to himself and yet proving his masculinity before an audience. A further advantage is that these women are not apt to be too demanding, either sexually or emotionally. His poverty as a male remains undetected.

Narcissistic men pay a great deal of attention to their appearance and, superficially, they are often very attractive. But the reputation they have of being great lovers is based on the quantity of their conquests rather than on the quality of their performance. A Don Juan will always arouse the curiosity of women and if, having given in to him, they are disappointed, they will not be in any hurry to spread the news.

Nevertheless, the reputation is not always ill-founded. Spurred on by vanity, some of these men—among them, my patient, Charles—do exhibit what seems like superior prowess. Worried about the possibility of premature ejaculation, a not uncommon failing in men of this type, Charles had trained himself to hold back to such an extent that he could prolong the sex act indefinitely. As a result, he boasted, women who had never had an orgasm before experienced it with him. The mechanism of the act being what it is, it is not surprising that—with increasing frequency as he grew older—he himself failed to achieve that culminating satisfaction.

Paradoxical as it may seem, sex is not really fun for the average Don Juan. Since he is morbidly concerned about the impression he is making, he cannot let go, abandon himself to the sheer pleasure of functioning.

Nor, on the whole, does he give much pleasure to his partners. His preoccupation with the question "How am I doing?" conveys itself in a lack of warmth, a sort of chilly *expertise*. Having perverted sex to a purpose for which it was never meant—exhibitionistic display— he sacrifices both its physical enjoyment and its capacity for creating an emotional bond. At the height of every adventure, he is still isolated and lonely.

Because the experience itself is so empty, so devoid of meaning and joy, he cannot tolerate a sustained relationship with any one woman. His only gratification lies in overcoming her resistance, in demonstrating once again "what a great boy am I." But, while the triumph soon withers, the anxiety remains. Like Alexander, he is driven from one conquest to another, spending the vital substance of his manhood for increasingly ephemeral gains.

Narcissistic personalities rarely seek help before they are totally depleted, at the end of their psychic resources. Their breakdowns are associated with profound depressions, paranoid states and a peculiarly stubborn kind of alcoholism. They may be so acutely disorganized that a period of hospitalization has to precede the initiation of psychotherapy. If they come earlier, like Charles, it is usually against their will, under the threat of divorce or of losing their jobs. Transference relationships are tenuous and the outlook not too hopeful. While these patients may be induced to give up the phantasy of gaining prestige through sexual conquests, their basic defect—the inability to relate in healthy terms to other people—is hard to overcome. The compulsive drive for prestige is merely shunted in a different direction, toward money or power or social ostentation. Though they love only themselves, they cannot love themselves unadorned. That is the saddest paradox of their natures.

Menopausal Type

Menopause is not simply a physical phenomenon, something that happens to women in middle age. It is also, for men as well as women, a state of mind, the realization—in some cases gradual, in others abrupt—that time is beginning to run out. There are certain men in whom the prospect of diminishing vigor, and particularly of diminishing sexual vigor, creates a sense of urgency so acute that they feel compelled to reverse the habits of a lifetime. In a last reckless adventure, or series of adventures, they try to retrieve what they have hitherto passed up—the immemorial masculine privilege of pursuing and possessing a variety of females. As seen in clinical practice, the men who conform to the menopausal type are, as a rule, highly active and successful with a record, up to this critical period, of complete marital fidelity.

Edward F. was a tycoon with a conscience. His career came straight out of Horatio Alger and so did his moral

principles. But not the agonizing predicament in which
he found himself. The Alger tradition does not take
sexual problems into account.

Edward's wife had recently discovered that, for the
past three years, he had been romantically involved
with another woman. Hurt and uncomprehending, she
had immediately offered to divorce him; if he loved
somebody else, she did not want to stand in his way.
But he could neither accept this solution nor give the
other woman up. He could only plead with his wife
to be patient, not to tell the children what he had
done, to give him time to think. He became so distraught that, at his wife's insistence, he agreed to seek
professional advice. So he arrived in my office, humiliated by his need for help but as unable to cope with the
situation as any schoolboy. In Edward's whole life—he
was then fifty-one—there had been only these two
women. As he put it, he felt married to them both.

Was Edward unhappy with his wife? Not at all.
There was an unusually close and affectionate bond
between them and their sexual relations had always
been satisfactory. What, then, had prompted his infidelity?

It all began, he said confusedly, at his daughter's wedding, a lavish affair very different from his own modest
nuptials. The whole courtship had been different, of
course, but somehow he hadn't thought of that before.
He compared himself unfavorably with his new son-in-
law, a demanding suitor who had literally taken his girl

by storm. Why, they had only known each other a few months! Edward, on the other hand, had grown up in the same town with his wife. She had been his mother's favorite piano pupil and often in the house, like a sister almost, interested in his inventions and encouraging him to do something about them. They got married when he sold his first patent. He was only twenty-two at the time and a virgin. So was she. They had always been very devoted to each other, very companionable. She had helped him a great deal in the early days; he was so shy that he probably would never have got started without her. If she left him, it would be like losing a part of himself.

I brought him back to the wedding. What had impressed him so much? Well, there was a kind of excitement about it, a romantic glow and fervor which he himself had never known. It made him feel old and sad, on the outside sort of. He couldn't really explain it but all he had accomplished in life—all his solid and enduring satisfactions—seemed meaningless in comparison. He looked at Ann, his wife, and wondered whether she felt the same way, that they'd missed something, something important.

Had he talked to her about it? No, there hadn't been an opportunity. And, the very next morning, a wire had summoned her to her father's bedside. He was gravely ill. She had been away for several weeks, the first time they'd been separated for more than a day or two at a time. With his daughter married, the boys

back in college and Ann not around either, he had been
very lonely. So, late one afternoon, after a board meet-
ing of one of his charities, he had asked this young
woman to have dinner with him. She was the publicity
director, very competent and attractive. They had gone
back to her apartment and, before he knew what he
was doing, he was making love to her. Her passionate
response had first stunned and then excited him to an
unbearable pitch. He still couldn't understand why a
wonderful girl like that should have fallen in love with
him. But she had and he couldn't let her down. Besides,
she made him feel grand. Though he didn't love her in
the way he loved Ann, it would kill him not to see her
any more.

Edward's young woman was far more experienced
than he was, completely uninhibited, clever and ambitious. She had set her cap for him because he was
rich and, apparently, manageable. Her sensual hold on
him was very great and she knew that he felt deeply
obligated to her. If, in this crisis, she had behaved with
the same consideration as his wife, he would undoubtedly have married her and been unhappy ever
after. Instead, she made furious scenes because he did
not immediately accept Ann's offer of a divorce and
overplayed her hand still further by refusing to let him
make love to her until the matter had been settled to
her satisfaction. In doing so, she released him from
bondage; Edward's sensuality did not survive the shattering of his romantic dream. He had not turned to

her primarily for sexual fulfillment. That he had, anyway. What he really wanted from her was a retouched image of himself—the portrait, glamorously highlighted, of a young and masterful male.

Why do solid sensible men like Edward indulge in such adolescent adventures? For a number of reasons, some dating far back in the past, others directly related to the position they have achieved.

They usually derive from a self-respecting family of limited economic status where the emotional atmosphere is warm and stable but where the textbook virtues are perhaps overemphasized while sex is barely acknowledged as a factor in life. There is often a dominant mother in the background—Edward was the only son of a widow who supported herself and her child by giving music lessons. Affectionate and moralistic, she set him an example of hard work, self-reliance and integrity. She also made him feel personally responsible for her happiness and welfare, a feeling which influenced his future attitudes not toward women alone but toward anybody in a relation of dependency to him.

A boy brought up in this way has many sources of ego strength and early develops a sense of his own worth. Sexually, however, he is shy and inhibited, partly as a result of childhood conditioning and partly because he has neither time nor money to spare for the social activities which accustom boys and girls to each other and train them for their differing sexual roles. The family emphasis on achievement keeps him busy at school-work, family chores and odd jobs of various kinds. He learns how to work, and work well, but not how to woo and win a girl. If he falls in love, it is from a distance; he is too diffident to make advances and he shrinks from competition. Like Edward, he simply slips into marriage with the first respectable girl who shows any interest in him. Almost invariably, she is as shy and inexperienced, as starved for romance, as he.

Their mutual dependency is, as a result, much greater than that of the average couple. So also, since they have much to make up for, is their desire to get on in the world. Husband and wife are a team, drawing strength from each other, cheerfully sacrificing temporary pleasures to assure a better future for themselves and their children. United in a common struggle, they develop a relationship of intimacy and trust which not only strengthens the man's belief in himself but allows him to concentrate his energies on economic advancement. They may have some sexual difficulties in the beginning but, as their bond is so close, they usually work out a fairly satisfactory adjustment. The man's anxiety on this score is reduced to a minimum; with no need to impress his wife, he can set his own pace and his eventual prowess may far outstrip that of his more experienced contemporaries. The trouble is that he has no way of knowing this. Aggressive and forceful in all that relates to his profession or business, he has never once demonstrated these qualities in his relations with women.

Such a man may reach his forties without having made a significant courtship advance of any kind. His inadequacy in this field has probably been rankling, consciously or unconsciously, for many years. In his slow rise to economic power, he has been surrounded by men who do not share his inhibitions and whose sexual adventures point up his own lack of experience. Not bound, as he is, by their marital vows, they go carousing together periodically or, as lone wolves, make the best of any likely opportunity. He becomes aware from their bantering or boastful talk—in which he cannot participate—that he has been excluded from what appears to him increasingly a desirable area of male activity. His position may be more exalted than theirs but, in this particular race, he has never even left the starting-post.

Gradually, his competitive impulses are aroused. Having succeeded against odds in the economic sphere, he feels the need to assert himself sexually, to prove that here, too, he can be as aggressive as his peers. His determination may be fortified by some incipient concern about diminishing potency or, as in Edward's case, by envy of the hectic courtships and the relative sexual freedom of his maturing children. The belated desire to demonstrate sexual mastery as well as the uneasiness and the vague regrets are symptoms of psychic menopause. The infidelity to which they so often lead is not a natural expression of sexual interest but a compulsive act, the fairly predictable end result of tensions which have been accumulating for a lifetime and finally explode.

He is no longer stayed, as he might once have been, by loyalty to his wife. While he has been consolidating his position in the world of affairs, the ties between them have slowly, almost imperceptibly, loosened. The woman who was formerly his partner, to whom he invariably turned for counsel and support, has dwindled in her importance to him. Where before she was a necessary prop, she is now only the chief beneficiary of his efforts, one among the many people who depend on him. His achievements give him all the confidence he needs and he is further bolstered by the adulation and respect his eminence inspires. He is subtly irked by the fact that his wife "knew him when"—more particularly if, in an attempt to maintain the basis of their original bond, she continually reminds him of his humble beginnings. While she may be proud of him and pleased with his accomplishments, he cannot help feeling that, in comparison with the prestige he commands outside the home, her appreciation of him is distinctly limited. Or, even more damaging to their relations, she may have failed to match his growth and be incapable of sharing the larger interests which now absorb him. Measured against the career women with whom he comes in daily contact, she seems narrow and unstimulating.

A complicating factor in men of this type is that they often have unacknowledged dependency needs. Their very success has placed them in a position where they are always, psychologically as well as financially, on the giving end of a relationship. While the role may gratify their self-esteem, it drains them emotionally; the part of them that has never grown up wants a bosom to lean on, an understanding mother to pat them on the head. That is why, when they get ready to plunge into an extramarital affair, they are so frequently attracted by the brisk and competent career woman. For one thing, she is sophisticated enough to recognize their frustrated yearnings and, for purposes of her own, to play their childish game of pursuit and capture. For another, her apparent self-sufficiency is a welcome change for the man who has begun, consciously or unconsciously, to resent the excessive demands made upon him by his environment. Unfortunately, a great many of these women have buried dependency needs themselves. Sometimes, they are simply on the make for a wealthy protector, sometimes they, too, become genuinely involved. In either case, they are determined to take permanent possession of the man they have snared. Once they have reduced him to a state of dependency, they pull out all the stops—from heart-broken tears to threats of leaving him or of suicide—in their effort to break up his marriage. Instead of the permissive mother he was looking for, he has a hysterical child on his hands. That is one of the oddest paradoxes we encounter in menopausal infidelity.

There are others. In a man so conditioned, the habit

of responsibility is hard to break. Having adopted, as he thinks, an aggressive masculine stance, he cannot run away from the obligations he has assumed. Torn by the conflicting claims of wife and mistress, afraid to lose either or both, his hard-won confidence collapses and an unbearable sense of guilt takes its place. Sooner or later, the affair comes to light—anything so explosive is hard to keep under cover—and the shattered lover winds up in an analyst's office. While he may be ashamed, as Edward was, by his need for help, he generally welcomes what seems to him like a respite from battle. Asking all parties to stand by, he looks for some magical solution from the analyst.

The therapeutic task is enormously complicated. With the exposure of his infidelity, the man's defenses break down completely. Flooded by guilt, he sinks into a pathological depression which deprives him of the courage and will-power so necessary for effective treatment. He may simultaneously develop functional disorders. In the severe and protracted conflict between his competitive drive and his unresolved dependency needs, he has strained his psychic resources to the utmost. Syndromes associated with over-mobilization—duodenal ulcer and hypertension—indicate the price that his body has paid.

Morevoer, his hope for a respite is illusory. The analytic couch is no refuge from the pressures assailing him; wife and mistress still vie with each other, in his mind if not in actuality. As far as the objective situation is concerned, the wife is usually readier to step out of the picture than the mistress. The latter is apt to be self-righteous and, on occasion, vindictive. In salvagable cases like Edward's, her untoward assumption of the wifely role has the paradoxical effect of leading him back to his real wife and a new beginning. If she wins out, her triumph more often than not is short-lived; in the pattern of mutual destructiveness which has been generated, the forced marriage breaks up. The former mistress may console herself with a fat settlement or alimony. The man is left with nothing.

The basic paradox of menopausal infidelity lies in the man's hopeless attempt to set back a clock which has already begun to run down. His adolescent dream of sexual romance and conquest cannot be fulfilled in middle age; the conditions which make it possible no longer exist. A mature and successful man does not stir the same emotions as a reckless, still uncommitted boy nor is he capable of feeling what that boy feels. When he tries, belatedly, to make up the void in his life, he does not find the response he craves. He only appeals to the acquisitive impulses of a calculating woman or, at sorry best, to the frantic need for reassurance of a frustrated one. He himself cannot transfer his striving for mastery into a sphere for which his whole conditioning has unfitted him without destroying the basis of his self-esteem and, possibly, the position he has built up at such great cost.

In the pungent words of Ecclesiastes: "To every

thing there is a season, and a time to every purpose under the heaven."

Romantic-Intellectual Type

By the time I met Gregory H., his marriage was already on the rocks. It had, I soon discovered, been drifting in their direction from the very beginning but, in the last six months or so, a strong wind of emotion had accelerated its course. Gregory, to put it plainly, had fallen in love with another woman. A girl, rather, one of his students. Gregory, a not untalented composer, was on the faculty of a local music school.

It was his wife, Fran, who originally consulted me. She arrived at my office in tears, desperate because he had asked her for a divorce and wondering what, if anything, she could do about it. She was crazy about him, she said, and their marriage had been wonderful, the real thing. For twelve years they had been wrapped up in each other, meant everything to each other. And now this. She simply couldn't understand how it was possible. The girl was so unattractive, too, a pale wispy little creature, almost morbidly shy, whom nobody in his senses would look at twice. Fran herself, I might add, was very attractive, a warm and glowing woman in her middle thirties who appeared much younger than her age.

When I pressed her for details, she said that the blow was utterly unexpected. Susan, the girl involved, had been underfoot quite a bit but, then, she lived nearby and, anyway, Fran had never dreamed that her husband could be interested in such a pathetic specimen, much less that he had been sleeping with her for some time. The whole story came out when she announced that at last they had enough money in the bank to start raising a family. Fran, who worked in a social agency, had been saving most of her salary for that purpose. She had expected Gregory to be delighted but instead he told her, with brutal candor, that he didn't want a baby and he didn't want her either. What he would like her to do with the money was to get a divorce so he could marry Susan. As Fran described that first scene and the even more destructive ones that followed, I realized that, whatever she felt about their marriage, it had not been a happy one for Gregory. The venom he poured out on her had obviously been accumulating for years.

He confirmed this when, in order to hurry up the divorce, he agreed to talk the matter over with me. Highly disturbed as he was, there was nothing about him to indicate a brutal nature. The mild and thoughtful face, the quiet voice belonged to a man who lived much in his mind. So did his choice of words. He made it clear at once that intervention was hopeless. He had had enough. If Fran refused to divorce him, he would leave her anyway. She was, he said, a formidable and

frightening person, like a tidal wave in her impact. If
he hadn't been so beaten, he would have run away from
her long before.

Yes, of course, he had been in love with her but that
was a long time ago and it was hard to remember now
what he had once felt about her. Or why he had felt it.
That compelling vitality of hers had bowled him over,
he supposed. As it still did, though in a quite different
way. Even thinking about her gave him a feeling of op-
pression. Too bad she couldn't see that the only thing
to do, in the circumstances, was to call the marriage
quits and start over. . . . Knowing this other girl,
Susan, had made him understand what a man really
wanted in a woman. She was so gentle and undemand-
ing and, at the same time, so curiously in accord with
him, like a thought in his own mind. . . . Had Fran
been demanding? Gregory's face darkened. Intolerably
demanding. She had drained him dry. He never felt
right any more, he could barely summon up the ambition to meet his classes. And he hadn't composed
anything worthwhile in years. It was her fault and yet
she kept after him, pushing, pounding, never leaving
him alone. Really, though he hated to say it—well, he
wouldn't say it but no doubt I knew what he meant.

Gregory's bitterness was corroding, implacable. Origi-
nating in sexual panic, too long unacknowledged, it had
been growing deep inside him like a cancer—destroying, along with his self-esteem, the love he had once
felt for his wife. It was too late, I decided, to save this

marriage even had he been willing, as he was not, to explore the real reasons for its failure. But it was not too late to help Fran. In further talks with her, I corroborated the impression I had gained from Gregory's violent language that here was another instance of the damage which may result when a couple's sexual relationship follows the erroneous pattern of the marriage manuals.

Neither of them, as it happened, had ever read any of the manuals. They didn't have to. They were "modern" young people, highly educated and enfranchised, at home in the twentieth century. The ideas of Havelock Ellis and his successors infused the atmosphere in which they moved, seeping into their minds by a kind of intellectual osmosis. For people who inhabit this particular cultural bailiwick, marriage centers on love and love on a highly romanticized concept of sex. They accept, without question, the postulates on which the manuals are based—the woman's right to a satisfying sexual experience and the man's obligation to see that she gets it. A loving husband will not seek orgastic fulfillment without attempting to assure it to his wife; his gratification is incomplete unless she shares it in full measure. The goal of the relationship, its culminating ecstasy, is mutual simultaneous orgasm.

In an earlier chapter, I discussed in detail the mistaken assumptions which underlie this ideal. While its recognition of female sexuality is praiseworthy, the burden it places on the man is well-nigh intolerable.

His limitations are ignored and so is the difference in orgastic pattern between the sexes. The husband who takes his "responsibilities" seriously is bound to run into trouble. He might as well reach for the moon. It is hardly less attainable than the goal of the manuals and he will not wreck his sexual mechanism in the process.

Gregory married Fran when they were both in their early twenties. Since he was young and virile and her response to him was ardent, they maintained for some years an enviable pitch of romantic excitement. Fran's initial shyness was also a help; though she welcomed his advances, she could not make any of her own, thus allowing Gregory to set the pace for their intercourse. Instead of appreciating his luck, however, he began after a while to get worried. Inordinately anxious to please, he wondered whether he was really satisfying Fran. Perhaps she was merely putting on a show for his benefit. One night, harried by doubts, he lost his erection. He was so upset about it that Fran, forgetting her shyness, went all out to reassure him. It was the beginning of a fundamental change in their relationship.

As time went by, Gregory became increasingly dependent and unsure of himself. More and more often, it was Fran who made the advances, he who responded. Meanwhile, with his potency diminishing, he developed a marked hypochondria, seeking refuge in illness from what he was later to interpret as her excessive demands. Yet, according to Fran, they had never been as close as in these final years of their marriage. It is probable that he had no more idea than she did of the bitterness he was unconsciously nourishing.

A situation of this kind lays the groundwork for infidelity. When a man's aggression collapses, his desire does, too. Intercourse with his wife is no longer a pleasure but a disagreeable duty which he may or may not be able to fulfill. Her sexual organs seem to him like a dangerous pit into which he must periodically venture at the risk of his manhood. And the more dependent he is on her otherwise, the more galling is his sense of inadequacy.

Such a man may have no intention of being unfaithful. But, driven by the need to restore his sexual confidence, he begins to seek the companionship of other women, at first perhaps on a purely friendly or professional basis. They are, almost invariably, women who share his interests, with whom he can talk about himself and his work. After a period of mutual exploration, the inevitable happens; he "falls in love." Impelled by an excitement which he had almost forgotten, he regains the initiative of which his marriage had deprived him. He discovers that he can function as well as he ever did. That discovery endears the woman to him still further. It also alienates him from his wife whom he can now hold responsible for his previous plight. The only difference, of course, is that he is again in active pursuit and that, for the moment at least, he is concentrating on his own pleasure.

None of the other patterns of infidelity is as destructive to the marital relation as this one. While the affair may be hidden for a while, the husband's total involvement will sooner or later force it to light. All the hostility he has been burying then vents itself upon his unfortunate wife in outbursts which are sometimes pathological in their cruelty. Remember how Gregory chose a moment of tender revelation to tell Fran that he wanted nothing more to do with her? He might have put off his announcement, led up to it gradually, softened his rejection in any number of ways. But he preferred to hit, and hit hard, when she was most vulnerable, thus paying her back with compound interest for the deficiencies in himself of which she had involuntarily made him conscious.

Naturally, these romantic lovers do not admit to such unflattering motives. And, since theirs is a pattern of intellectuals, they are usually able to rationalize their behavior with considerable effectiveness. It is the wife whose deficiencies are emphasized, who is made to feel guilty. She may be called insatiable, as Fran was, or charged with frigidity; depending on circumstances, she is either insensitive to the things of the spirit or too competitive with her husband in his own sphere of cultural activity.

But the most subtle and devastating rationalization of all is the one which derives from the very nature of their original bond. To the romantic, marriage is a prolonged honeymoon or nothing. If one accepts the premise that the sex act is degrading unless it is the expression of romantic love, then one obviously should not engage in it when one is no longer in love. If the wife protests that, for her part, she *is* in love, the erring husband has a ready answer. They have always agreed, have they not, that the feeling must be mutual? Affection does not count nor do the ordinary decencies of interpersonal behavior. A man like Gregory, in contrast to our other types, is totally incapable of accepting the sexual impulse in its own right. His most distinguishing feature is his need to fall in love to justify his sexual advances or to account for his new-found sexual competence.

An unhappy aspect of the situation is that, profoundly alienating as it is and hurtful to both partners, they may be forced to continue living with each other because, economically, they have no alternative. That is particularly true where children are involved. Under present conditions, it takes a good deal of money to go through with a divorce and support two separate households and a man of this type is usually engaged in the kind of intellectual or creative work which does not pay high financial dividends. Not that, where he is concerned, it really matters too much. The pattern which drove him to infidelity repeats itself in any subsequent marriage.

It is worthwhile remarking at this point that one of the most striking paradoxes of romantic infidelity is the marked similarity in the man's object choices. The new woman is usually a pretty close approximation of the wife he rejects. Gregory's case may seem to contradict this statement but his self-loathing was by then so great that he may have found it hard to approach any woman who was too obviously desirable. There is no doubt, moreover, that Susan's shyness woke echoes of Fran as she was in the early days of their marriage, before his anxiety had caused the relationship to deteriorate. In any case, we have only Fran's testimony that the girl was unattractive and she was not, in the circumstances, an unprejudiced witness.

Another paradox is that a man of this sort, for all his romantic over-valuation of sex, still shrinks from accepting it on its own terms. Physical compatibility— the imperative of the body which unhesitatingly recognizes and seeks out its mate—is not his primary concern. He always has to find an excuse, preferably an intellectual one, for becoming interested in a woman. She has a fine mind, she understands him, they speak the same language, etcetera, etcetera.

It is probable that the man's sexual drive is not too strong to begin with. An investigation of his premarital background is apt to reveal limited experience of actual intercourse. Heavy necking and petting, to the point of mutual orgasm, is substituted for the genital act. While he justifies such limited intercourse on the grounds of consideration for the woman, it is usually in accord with his own unconscious wishes. Even in marriage, the pregenital play assumes more significance than the act itself. The stress on affectionate fore-play is an attempt to discount, in advance, the potential failure of his genital apparatus. Many of these men do not enter the woman until they have satisfied her by clitoral stimulation.

In analyzing the romantic male, the most important therapeutic task is to reverse his tendency toward passivity. The fear of castration which underlies it—a factor in his exaggerated need to placate the woman—is made clear to him by a reconstruction of its original source. Sometimes that insight into his unconscious motivations is enough to restore him to healthy function and to establish his marriage on a sounder foundation. But it is my impression that, in addition to the purely analytical work, he requires some degree of re-education to undo the impact of the marriage manuals and of the cultural atmosphere in which their conceptions thrive.

What conclusions can we draw from this rather schematized discussion of the unfaithful male as seen in New York City and its environs? Let me first repeat what I said earlier: there are probably as many motives for infidelity as there are individual personality structures. In other words, every case of infidelity is, in certain respects at least, a special case. If I have dealt with only four and concentrated in each on its *typical* aspect, it is because no problem can be handled scientifically unless some attempt is made to disentangle that which is general in it from that which is specific.

This particular problem has been relatively neglected. Infidelity has either been condemned, without more ado, on a strictly moralistic basis or complacently accepted as a normal protest against the restrictions of monogamy. (According to Kinsey's statistics, fifty per cent of all married men in America have been unfaithful at one time or another.) In analytical studies of the subject, the tendency has been to dispose of it with such overdrawn and all-inclusive clichés as unconscious homosexuality, Casanova complex, unfulfilled oedipal strivings and the like. Yet it is important to keep the basic types of infidelity separated. In each, quite distinct psychodynamic factors are operative and none of them can be understood completely without some reference to the varying social and economic background. From the point of view of therapy, these differences are significant.

Is infidelity ever normal? I indicated, at the very beginning of this chapter that there are certain circumstances where it is—where, indeed, a too rigid fidelity would itself be suspect. Let us also admit that, in many instances, it is the safety-valve which prevents a marriage from coming to grief. But it is not going too far to say that, when it follows the compulsive pattern exhibited by any of the four major types I have described, it is not only destructive in its effects on the marriage but self-destructive as well. And self-destruction must be our ultimate criterion of normality even in this most complex of social phenomena. For the man who does not hurt himself in the course of extramarital activity rarely hurts those about him.

CHAPTER 8

The Outer Limits:

Paradoxes of the Search for Freedom

Freedom . . . a concept seldom clearly defined, a dream without specific content which is, nevertheless, among the most powerfully motivating forces in human conduct. What *do* we mean by freedom? The dictionary definitions are endless but, in one way or another, they all imply an unshackling, a state in which bonds have been cast off and the organism concerned—an individual, a group, a class, a nation—is able to do what it wants or needs to do.

Conscientious people interpret the term with scrupulous care; it means for them the opportunity to think and act in accord with the dictates of an inner monitor which they fondly associate with all that is good and decent in life. For other more arrogant temperaments, freedom is the equivalent of the golfer's shouted "Fore!," clearing the way of everything that might impede their progress or otherwise interfere with their desires. In this category, we encounter both leaders of men and criminals; it all depends on the goals they have set for themselves.

When the dream of freedom is renounced, existence becomes meaningless, a "weary, stale, flat and unprofitable" business, something to be endured rather than experienced, the negation of life. But only children, and the kind of revolutionaries who remain children at heart, expect to see the dream translated into uncompromising fact. As the philosopher Santayana observes in one of his wise and penetrating essays: "Absolute liberty . . . is impracticable; it is a foolish challenge thrown by a new-born insect buzzing against the universe; it is incompatible with more than one pulse of life. All the declarations of independence in the world will not render anybody really independent." *

That is the first paradox of freedom. Another, more subtle, more disillusioning, is that the struggle for freedom, if pursued too exclusively, may be self-defeating, resulting in more severe impediments than those

* George Santayana, "English Liberty in America," from "Character and Opinion in the United States." New York, Charles Scribner's Sons, 1920.

which it seeks to remove. There is nobody as enslaved as the fanatic, the person in whom one impulse, one value, has assumed ascendency over all others. And it is sad but true that this degeneration into fanaticism is an occupational hazard for those most dedicated to the cause of freedom. The cobwebby net is of their own fashioning but it is no less constricting for that.

The psychiatrist sees many people who are caught in such self-woven traps. He is also more aware than others, perhaps, of the limitations to freedom set by nature and society. Yet, paradoxically, it is a major part of his job to "free" the suffering human beings who come to him from the many entanglements, both internal and external, which prevent them from functioning in a healthy manner or indeed, on occasion, in any manner at all. The dilemma which confronts him confronts us all; it involves the very conditions for individual survival, the terms by which the human creature may accomodate itself to a world it never made but must, perforce, inhabit.

Let us define, then, as sharply as we can, the nature of the freedom possible to man, the boundaries beyond which it cannot reach without damage to him and the satisfactions he may find by voluntarily keeping within them instead of seeking vainly to break them down. The boundaries, while interlocking, are of three kinds and it will clarify our definition to consider them separately. We shall discuss the problem of freedom, then, in terms of man as a *biological organism;* in terms of his *early development in a family setting;* and, finally, in terms of his relationship to the *larger society* of which he is part.

Biologically, man is an animal, a living thing which moves and feels, marvellously intricate in its bodily mechanism, gross in its needs and blindly intent on preserving its position in nature. Man's most fundamental aim, in other words, is the same as that of his animal kin—to survive and to reproduce, and to do so, incidentally, in the most favorable environment he can find for himself. It is his aim and his right, the most basic of all; a society which disregards it does so at its peril. To offer a man the vote while denying him that right is a cruel joke, a travesty of freedom. He will not appreciate the privilege, he will use it for revenge, as we have observed to our sorrow on more than one occasion.

But to be well-fed, well-housed and clothed is not enough; man is also a *feeling* creature, with a complex central nervous system which provides pathways for the expression of his emotional reactions. Too often, and especially in advanced civilizations, emotional expression is blocked or distorted by educational influences and energy is turned back upon the body, which testifies to its outrage with a host of alarming psychosomatic disorders. A man may be "free" in the civilized sense of the word; his moral dignity may be unimpaired and his mind roam at will over the continents of thought.

Nevertheless, if he has lost his capacity to give way to rage and resentment, if his sexual impulses are hampered or deflected, if he cannot acknowledge pain and fear and grief and dependency, he has purchased those lofty freedoms at the price of others more vital to his animal constitution. Hypertension, ulcers and similarly unpleasant diseases are rarely met with in the more primitive and earth-bound cultures. They reflect a bad bargain made by civilization and their effect on the individual may well be catastrophic.

Man's biological endowment includes another faculty which, while not unique to him, is so highly developed, so "different," that it led the philosophers of ancient Greece to classify him as the "thinking animal." Perhaps they were rash, perhaps they exaggerated, but their point is well taken. Other animals have minds in the broad sense of the term, they even have, in a more or less rudimentary form, intelligence—which is the capacity for grasping a situation and adapting one's behavior accordingly. Their intelligence, indeed, occasionally seems more efficient than ours because it is linked directly to their primary needs and never diverted to extraneous goals. Those goals of man, how odd they are sometimes, how—we might almost say—unnecessary. That is the difference. Only in human beings is the intelligence "free," no longer simply an organ of survival but something brooding, creative and articulate which adds a new dimension to nature and often disdains it, forgetting its origin as the butterfly—

enraptured by the power of its wings, the heady scent of grass and flower, the whole sunlit universe—forgets the dark chrysalis in which it grew.

The artist starving in his garret, the scholar burning the midnight oil, the scientist intent upon an experiment which may end in his and the world's destruction —these have long been clichés, puppets through whom we symbolize a specifically human experience, so familiar to us that we tend to overlook its novelty in the life of nature. Many of our most admired virtues— heroism, devotion, a self-sacrificing loyalty to our species—we share with other animals. Intellectual virtue, however, "this strange uneasiness, this truant joy, which we call thought" * is ours alone and the fulfillment it may bring to dedicated individuals has no precedent.

Yet, as the work of Freud and his followers has shown, we *can* indulge this peculiar virtue without, in the process, wrecking our biological apparatus. Many of our impulses, among them the most primitive, are capable of transformation; the energy attaching to them in the unconscious is deflected from its original goals and thus made available for other and often more socially acceptable purposes. A young man, for instance, may have felt in his childhood profound hatred of a brother more favored than himself; by renouncing his hatred, turning his fury and rivalry in another direction, he may become an outstanding competitive athlete. The

* George Santayana, "The Psyche," from "Soliloquies in England and Later Soliloquies." New York, Charles Scribner's Sons, 1922.

same is true of worthy impulses which are prevented, for one reason or another, from finding outlet in reality. An involuntarily childless woman may compensate for her deprivation by adopting, as it were, a whole community, serving it with the unstinted passion she would have lavished on her baby; or a soldier, separated from his wife, may discover an unsuspected talent for painting or writing. The talent was there all the time, but until he diverted to it the force of his sexual energies, it remained unrealized.

Great artists, creative personalities in general, have other sources of energy. They have learned to tap deep underground springs, vestigial impulses no longer necessary to the race but still bubbling away in the depths of the mind. To the majority of people, they are forever inaccessible. Every healthy person, however, has the capacity to modify and defer satisfactions, to turn the energy of a particular impulse toward a substitute goal. This capacity makes civilization possible.

What we have been describing are unconscious processes, almost wholly beyond the control of our will. This is, in itself, no limitation, however, just as it is no limitation to be able to walk and talk and think without conscious effort. The fact that so much of our behavior is automatic, unconsciously regulated, is just what makes freedom possible for us. It releases great quantities of energy which then become available for voluntary activities and which can be drawn on when we meet, as we do daily, the complex challenges of an ever more

complex world. Our unconscious is like a vast sub-
terranean factory with intricate machinery that is never
idle, where work goes on day and night from the time
we are born until the moment of our death. It does the
menial work of our organism, the routine tasks which
would otherwise enslave our attention.

But there is a paradox here, too. The same unconscious which gives us our freedom can also take it away
from us. Psychoanalysis has perhaps unduly emphasized
the conflicts in unconscious processes and the fashion in
which infantile conditioning disturbs man's aspirations
to freedom.

The *conditioning experiences of infancy* and early
childhood influence us to an extent hardly dreamed of
before the days of psychoanalysis. They constitute the
second important boundary to man's freedom and they
are a direct result of the fact that he is helplessly dependent for a much longer period than any other species of animal.

The human infant is the most vulnerable of all creatures. Compared with the young of other species, he
seems unfinished, appallingly unprepared for the hazards of existence. And so he is. Watch a new-born calf.
It is a competent little thing, tottering to its feet almost
instantly. Its legs are spindly and trembling but they
function, they take the calf where it wants to go. And
the marvellous thing is that it knows where to go and
what to do when it gets there. A few minutes after birth,

the calf has found its mother's teats and is suckling contentedly. Nobody has to teach it anything, it is informed by instinct.

The baby has no such unerring guide. Not only is it physically incapable of reaching the breast on its own; it even has to be shown what the breast is for. It has to learn practically everything it needs for survival, an educational process of many years' duration, requiring the constant presence, as protectors and teachers, of a variety of adults, among whom the mother and father, or their substitutes, are of course preeminent. Unlike the calf, which is so nearly self-sufficient, which needs its mother very briefly and its father not at all, the baby develops successfully only in a family setting.

The advantage would appear to be on the side of the calf. But this is true, if it is true, only at the beginning of life. Instinct, while sure and swift, is inflexible; it places a gross limitation on development. Where it governs wholly, as in insects, there is no choice for the individual, no possibility of change, merely a pattern of existence endlessly repeated from one generation to the next. The human being, on the other hand, coming into the world unfinished, with a minimum of instinctual equipment, has an enormous plasticity. It is, as his career on earth proves, a valuable asset.

Plasticity is greatest during infancy and childhood. In those years, we are literally molded by our environment, in particular the emotional environment created by our parents. Our need of them is so great, our desire to remain in their good graces so strong, that we renounce, in their favor, our immoderate childish passions and incorporate into ourselves not only what they teach us but what they are, their unconsidered moods as well as their most stringent pronouncements. Our parents' attitudes become ours; converted into an internal regulatory system, a sort of watchdog, they remain permanently ensconced in the depth of our personalities. That is the superego, the most powerful component in the assemblage of qualities popularly known as "character." While it may be modified to a certain extent, it is basically resistant to change and its influence is felt in everything we do and say and think and believe. There is no question that, by predisposing us to certain definite patterns of behavior, it limits our freedom. In extreme cases, where the ghostly voice of the parents is too harsh, too demanding, it may destroy the capacity for pleasure, for work, for independent choice, for mature activity in general.

Nevertheless, the superego is an indispensable acquisition, both for the individual and for mankind as a whole. It is the source of our morals and ideals, of everything we lump together when we speak of the "higher" side of human nature; it is what differentiates us from the beasts in the jungle whose savage impulses we share and would indulge as fiercely were it not for the existence of that watchdog within us. In a larger sense, it is the repository and representative of tradition, the acquired values of the race, painfully accumulated in the course of man's long and checkered history. Without such a mechanism for the transmittal of values from one generation to another, there would be no civilization, no culture, no history. In human beings, the superego takes over some of the function of instinct in animals, while adding to it special functions of its own. It is at once the latent memory and the conscience of mankind.

And—this must be emphasized—it can only be formed successfully by means of family relationships. We have learned at some cost that the absence of a family unit or its premature breakdown may permanently damage a child's development and its future adjustment to society. Even an inadequate home is probably better than none at all. That is why we now make every effort to find a foster home for children whom death or some other cause has deprived of their natural families. An orphan asylum, no matter how well run, cannot provide the setting for that intense and intimate drama through which the child, as it were, practices his humanity and learns to find his place in the world. He learns *through* his dependency, that is the paradox. It is his abject need—for love and approval no less than for protection—that makes him curb impulses as wild and peremptory, as dangerous, as any tiger's. It is his need that socializes him.

Society, when finally he becomes an active part of it, puts still further limitations on his freedom. It is the last great boundary and the one of which, on the whole, he is most conscious. If, in spite of all his conditioning, he is still rebellious, it is usually society that he rebels *against*. Some men, philosophers or artists, construct their own private universe to escape its insistent demands; they may even take to the woods like Thoreau or go to Tahiti like Gauguin. Others, more given to direct action, will become revolutionaries or criminals. Their rebellion may be unconsciously directed against a father or mother image, or against their own inadequacy, but it is society they indict and that feels their sting.

Every society that has ever existed, from the most primitive to the most advanced, necessarily restricts its members to a greater or less degree. The areas of restriction vary, sometimes radically, between one culture and another and between groups in the same basic culture. These differences are wholesome; they prevent values from solidifying; they lead to comparison, competition, migration. And, fortunately, there will always be healthy nonconformists to point out these differences, draw conclusions from them, winning by their efforts another outpost of freedom here and there. Among them will be boldly creative personalities like Christ or Moses who add new values to the common stock of humanity.

Essentially, however, society is a fellowship, a sharing of vital interests, and its restrictions, as far as the average person is concerned, are not too galling. If they coincide closely enough with those which his superego imposes, he may not even be conscious of them. Certainly he is unable to realize the degree to which he conforms to a common cultural image. What he sees are the vast number of individual differences between him and his fellows. The sameness of what Kardiner calls the basic personality structure is perceived only by the foreigner, the outsider, who is similarly unaware of the uniformities in his own culture.

This unconscious identity among its members is the cement that holds a society together. The people who live in it start out with common assumptions and seek compatible goals, thus avoiding the chaotic break-downs, sometimes leading to civil war, which afflict a society riven by fundamental disagreements. And since they speak, as we say, the same emotional language, they are able to communicate easily, almost without words, the expressive grimace or gesture conveying meaning as readily as speech. This kind of communication is on a much deeper level than intellectual understanding. Because it is not susceptible to distortion, it *relates* people to each other and serves as a buffer against the sense of isolation, probably the most terrifying of all human experiences.

Primitive societies have always recognized this terror. Isolation, or ostracism, means death to them and they use it to punish offenders. The custom—and the dread as well—survives in our prison mores where to be put "in solitary" is the severest punishment meted out to criminals. But too many of us, in more emancipated societies, become our own jailers. Seeking freedom, we break tie after tie. We try to be independent of others, self-sufficient beyond the limits of normal tolerance. As often as not, we end up in a state of profound depression, the psychological equivalent of the solitary cell.

How much freedom *can* we tolerate? And how much can society permit us without endangering itself? These are not academic questions today. As our knowledge of other cultures expands, we become increasingly aware that our standards and codes are by no means universal. Ways of life divergent from our own, and often incompatible, have their passionate partisans, too. Our values shift under our feet like quicksand. We begin to focus, not on the successes of our society, but on its failures, both real and imagined. The great truth of human nature—that, to live at all, one must make choices and stick to them—is tossed on the garbage heap.

Many people, and especially young people, are incapable of choosing when confronted with too many alternatives. Or they choose badly, on impulse, and then try to reverse themselves. In either case, the result is bewilderment, indecision and intolerable disorder. Their plight is analogous to the infant's whose parents deny him the guidance he craves. Society is a kind of parent to its members. If it, and they, are to thrive, its values must be clear, coherent and generally acceptable. There are decisions, involving the community as a whole, that are too agonizing to be made independently.

In conditions of health, they are determined by unconscious identification.

Some societies are so sick or so confused that identification of this kind becomes impossible to the majority of their members. And there are individuals who cannot, in any case, achieve it. The person who is always out of tune, who complains that he is being stifled by the limitations of his culture, that it denies him satisfaction, is usually unable to find satisfaction anywhere. A deep-seated character disturbance isolates him from his kind; they seem strangers to him and he frets at the fate that placed him among them. His desperate cries for freedom are not meaningless, however. What he needs, and unconsciously seeks, is freedom from himself.

Let me recapitulate. Absolute freedom is an illusion, a mirage always beckoning from afar. Its green trees and running streams do not exist and, if we wish to be content on this earth, we should not let the vision of them beguile us too much. Within the boundaries set for us, we can move around with relative ease. But, if wanting more, wanting the impossible, we force those boundaries, there are new and more difficult obstacles in our path. The enchanting vision is no closer, it is farther away than before.

For centuries men believed, as many of them still do, that there was a solution to the dilemma. Freedom, they agreed, could not be attained in this world. But

how about the next? There it has another name, paradise, but its meaning is the same—utter fulfillment.
The angelic hosts have no bodies to trip them up, they
are not hampered by nagging bonds. They are free.

Religion—by the hope it gave, the promise of an
eventual if long deferred satisfaction—reconciled count-
less millions to the frustrations they encountered in life.
But, in our day, its consolations are not enough. Men
seek fulfilment here and now.

How, by what means? Largely, in recent times,
through themselves, their individual capacities and
drives. To those who did not understand them too well,
the original findings of depth psychology seemed to
sanction such an ideal. Inhibition, not indulgence, was
the devil. Children were encouraged to express themselves, to vent their talents and impulses indiscriminately. Sexual prudery was more frowned upon than
sexual excess. There was an exhilarating feeling that
"doing what comes naturally" would make everybody
happier and healthier.

Has it? Let us examine some of the things people do
naturally and what happens to them in the process.
There is sex, for instance, and making lots of money
or otherwise winning power and prestige. For a minor-
ity, but a growing one, there is exercising one's mind to
the utmost, experimenting, criticizing, creating or just
thinking. These are among the activities by which
people measure their freedom to be themselves.

Sexual freedom sounds wonderful. It feels wonderful, too—for a time, anyway. But then, sooner or later, it begins to pall. Women, being closer to their own needs, usually discover this quicker than men. They realize that, as a substitute for marriage, it is pretty poor pickings and that, if they are married, it poisons what might have been a good relationship, a good home. Marrying again doesn't solve the problem either, not if the breakup came from playing around. Somehow they keep on making the same mistakes. Sexual adventures may come to be only a bad habit, not a joy at all, or a joy so fleeting that it is hardly remembered. What *is* remembered is the boredom, the disgust, the feeling of waste. And then there are the children. They may not know exactly what is going on but they sense something inimical, threatening to themselves, and they grow moody and suspicious, sometimes openly alarmed. If divorce tears up the family, they are desperately unhappy. Whoever wins, they lose.

Men and women have begun to recognize that sexual freedom is not the answer to their emotional problems. The false values of the last twenty or thirty years are becoming less prevalent; sober second thought is taking the glamor out of infidelity. The advantage, for both partners, of a long-range stable relationship is acknowledged, if not always acted upon. And there is an increasing sense of responsibility toward children, a determination to make a good job of being parents. That alone is a powerful inducement for monogamy. It is not an easy institution to maintain. Where social pressures are lacking, self-control must take their place.

The gradual shift in sexual values is apparent even in highly sophisticated circles, where it is due largely to the spread of psychiatric insights. The realization is dawning that habitual infidelity is not so much the mark of a free soul as a symptom of psychic maladjustment. A case in point is that of a forty-one-year-old man who came to me as a patient not long ago. He was, he told me, in the midst of divorce proceedings. The divorce would be his third but he intended to marry again and he wanted the next marriage to stick. That was why he was seeking analytic treatment.

This man had been living for many years in the kind of milieu that used to be called "bohemian." All his friends and associates were creative personalities, intensely interested in their work and thoroughly uninhibited. While he was telling me about them, he suddenly interrupted himself. About that new marriage he was planning—maybe it should be different from the others. Maybe he should pick out a wife who would be faithful to him. That had never happened before and it would be an interesting experience. Before I could say anything, he burst out with a singularly revealing statement. "You know, doctor," he said. "I'd like to go even further. I'd like to try being faithful myself."

Creative people, like this patient, are often bemused by the belief that ordinary standards of conduct do not apply to them, that they are somehow different from other human beings. And so they are, to a degree. Their psychic makeup is such that they transgress, more readily than others, the boundaries which circumscribe the freedom possible to man. Compared with what is boiling inside them, nothing else seems of real importance. Perhaps they are right. But that does not mean they are exempt from the laws that govern human behavior. They suffer for their transgressions, sometimes to the point of losing the very creative power for which they have sacrificed so much.

No single faculty can be divorced from the totality of life without damaging life. Artists tend to forget this fact or, if they remember, to ignore it. The same is true, to an even greater extent, of pretentious "intellectuals." The passions of the mind, it sometimes seems, are more inordinate than those of the body. There is no doubt that intellect is man's supreme achievement as a species, the instrument by which he has gained control over other species and over nature itself. But it can be a dangerous instrument in the hands of an unstable personality. That razor-edged blade cuts deep and one of its victims may be the man who wields it.

Among our most difficult psychiatric cases are those people in whom intellect blooms like a parasitic flower at the expense of the organism as a whole. The organism itself, the plant, is sick. Patients of this sort often show a remarkable insight; they explore their unconscious with grim thoroughness and do not quail at the ugly things they find there. They do not quail because they have cut themselves off from all those early disturbing experiences by the process which we call rationalization. The tragic story they are telling no longer involves them. It has become the story of somebody else. Insights thus protected from the emotional response proper to them have no therapeutic effect. The patient's logic is triumphant. But he remains sick.

By losing contact with his own emotions, the intellectual may lose contact with other people as well. He cannot understand them and he cannot *relate* to them. That is the basis of the curious distrust with which he is so often regarded. His ideas, however brilliant, become suspect. He has forfeited his humanity and, with it, the influence which his great gifts should have won him.

There is another special type of the hag-ridden personality—the man who is obsessed by the idea of money and devotes his life to accumulating as much of it as he can. He is not an endearing character. In the first place, his goal is itself perverted; anyone who wants money so exclusively, either for its own sake or for the power it will give him over other people, is already deeply neurotic. To achieve his goal, moreover, he must be willing to engage in practices which are peculiarly damaging, both to himself and to others. Massive economic success puts a premium on such qualities as egoism, unscrupulous competitiveness and a general disposition to ride roughshod over obstacles, human or otherwise.

It would be bad enough if these qualities manifested themselves only in business matters. But that is rarely the case. Almost invariably, they are carried over into

the individual's personal relations where their effect
is deadly. Nobody can really be intimate with such a
character. There is no warmth in him, no give and take,
no human responsiveness. He cannot make friends and
even his family learns to shun him. The caricature of
the tycoon, sitting all by himself on his moneybags, is
not an exaggeration. It reflects his estrangement. If his
purpose was to "liberate" himself, he has succeeded
with a vengeance. But his efforts have landed him in a
much narrower and more constricting cell. For the
term of his life, he remains "in solitary." No escape is
possible for him. He himself has locked the door and
thrown away the key.

Without close human ties, without the warm ex-
change, the mutuality of feeling that comes from intimate associations, we are lost souls, sick with a loneliness that turns our dearest achievements to dust. We
need each other, and the need is of a depth unknown to
less protected species. The long dependency of our infantile years leaves behind it an ineradicable hunger—
for contact, for response, for love—and we should feel
no shame in admitting its force. It is satisfied most
completely in a family setting, where the basic configuration of our early experiences is subtly modulated to
accord with our changed position, but it may seek and
find outlets almost anywhere.

Some outlet there must be. That is true even of those
curious people who have apparently renounced personal fulfillment of any kind and thrown their energies

into an impersonal movement or "cause." Let no one think that they have succeeded in eliminating their dependent needs; they have only shifted them to an inappropriate channel. Such people are not altogether trustworthy. Though they may seem selflessly devoted, they have in fact made a neurotic transference and the cause for which they have abnegated so much may suffer as a consequence. They tend to be unstable, intolerant of their less committed associates, resentful when their activities are not appreciated, and too readily discouraged when they fail. What they want, though they may not know it, is to have the love they invest in the cause returned in full measure. A neurotic investment of this kind almost invites disillusionment. If it is sufficiently intense, they may end by breaking down or, turning renegade, attack what was once the object of their desire. They are the stuff of which martyrs are made and, for all their occasional usefulness, they are a problem to themselves and others.

When dependency is not recognized, it becomes distorted, narrowing the area of possible freedom. But over-dependence is a distortion, too. We have all known those persons—they are sometimes quite charming—who behave like grownup babies, and prove equally burdensome. They will not or cannot stand on their own feet; they are always looking around for support, attaching themselves to the nearest mother or father image they can find. Wholly dependent on their intimates, they manipulate them in the way children do, with cajolery, tears and a general aura of helplessness. Since they have never really established a separate identity, individual achievement means little to them and the broader concerns of their culture leave them cold. All they want is a bosom, sheltering arms, a hospitable knee. Freedom is something they know nothing of.

"To thine own self be true" is a wise admonition when the self is understood to be what in fact it is, an unbelievably complex focus of needs and drives which must be brought into balance, not only with each other but with the world outside the self. We are, as it were, in the center of an immense web, a series of interlocking relationships which range outward from the ego, through the intimate members of our family circle, our friends, our professional associates, to society at large and, finally, to humanity itself.

These relationships are not accidental, not alien to the self but an integral part of it, as necessary to its healthy functioning as the organs of its own body. Even the schizophrenic who has turned his back on life, who has retreated to the fastness of his secret being, populates that stony wilderness with the images—fragmentary, twisted, but still recognizable—of the real world he has abandoned.

We cannot exist in isolation and so, however various the patterns we create for ourselves, we cannot be altogether free. The claims made upon us, from within and without, are many; they jostle each other, competing for our loyalty and our attention. That is why we must learn to compromise to some extent, to limit our goals and accept, without feeling defrauded, partial satisfactions—that is, partial satisfactions in each of the three balancing forces which we have described in the beginning of this chapter as indispensable. "All or nothing" is an infantile slogan, a confession of megalomania, at once absurd and tragic in its implications. People whose personalities are in vital equilibrium do not make such an unregenerate demand. They acknowledge that "something" is not only as much as they can expect but may even be preferable as an indication that conflicting impulses—in themselves and in others—have achieved a kind of harmony. And, when every day brings something in the way of satisfaction, the result is happiness.